In memory of my dear husband,
Jack Milton

Widow

A Survival Guide for the First Year

Joanna Romer

To Helen,
with love
and gratitude,
Joanna
Dec. 1, 2013

For information, contact
MSI Press
1760-F Airline Highway, #203
Hollister, CA 95023

Cover designed by CDL Services

Library of Congress Control Number 2012945585

ISBN: 9781933455242

Table of Contents

Part One: Learning to Be Alone

1. Being Alone 3
2. Two Rules for Survival..9
3. Nurturing Yourself...15
4. Make a Plan 19
5. Tears..27
6. Friends 31
7. Cooking for One..37
8. The First Holiday..41
9. Prayer...45
10. Let People Help You...49
11. Journal Writing..53
12. The Value of Grief..57

Part Two: Learning to Take Care of Yourself

13. Rituals 65
14. Making Household Repairs...69
15. Lunching Out..73
16. Lists 77
17. Your Birthday 81
18. Loneliness 85
19 Facebook 89
20. You Will Make Mistakes 93
21. Your Looks...97
22. Dealing with Guilt.. 101
23. Money.. 105
24. Find a Project 109

Part Three: Learning to Enjoy Life Again

25. Healing.. 115

26. Maybe a Job 119

27. Memories 123

28. Sexual Fantasies 127

29. iPhone... 131

30. Your Health.. 135

31. Meditation 139

32. Confidence.. 143

33. Aging... 147

34. Cleaning out Hubby's Closet.................... 151

35. Photographs... 155

36. Survivor Guilt.. 159

Part Four: Learning to Be You

37. Wedding Ring... 165

38. How to Tell When You're Getting Better 167

39. Spontaneity and Changing Your Mind 171

40. Dating 177

41. Exercise... 181

42. His Birthday.. 185

43. Other Women's Husbands......................... 189

44. Dealing with the Thing
You Don't Want to Deal With 193

45. Travel 195

46. The Awakening.. 199

47. Sleeping on One Side of the Bed 203

48. Welcome to You!... 207

Appendix

25 Ways to Know You're Healed 211

New List of Nice Things to Do (2) 213

Accomplished in February 214

Accomplished in June 215

Things Yet to be Done 216

New List of Scrumptious Things to Do 216

List of Current Blessings (2) 217

Desires of the Heart 219

Index

.... 221

Part One: Learning to Be Alone

JOANNA ROMER

Chapter One

Being Alone

When I was in my mid-20s, I worked at *Cosmopolitan* magazine as an Assistant Editor. My tenure there was short (barely a year), but because my editor liked me I was able to secure freelance assignments in later years. Writing for *Cosmo*, I learned that almost any problem can be remedied with concentrated self-nurturing and a few well thought-out lists. And so, throughout the years, I was able to handle two divorces, three marriages, many job changes and the untimely deaths of both my parents (although this last occurrence required the help of a very nice therapist).

When Jack, my beloved husband of 16 years, died at the age of 71, I was devastated. There were days in those first months when I really didn't see what I had to live for. Other times, I believed that I too would soon leave this earth, and so I scampered around trying to get my affairs in order. If you are a recent widow, you're probably aware of both these stages.

Such feelings, fortunately, are usually transitory. With a little guidance from your wiser self, you can limit the time spent feeling like there is nothing to live for. As far as getting your affairs in order, this is actually a rather effective diversion from the early days of mourning, and strangely comforting, like cleaning up after a good party.

There are two important rules to consider right away, perhaps as early as the day following the memorial service.

The first is gratitude: be thankful for all the wonderful years you had with that lovely man. The second rule, equally as important, is to do something for someone else. By remembering all the good years, and occupying your time by thinking up ways to help others, you may find yourself getting through the first couple of weeks in relative calm.

The truth about being a widow is that you are forced to live in the moment. Each day calls for decisions the likes of which you've never had to make before, such as where you'll spend your first Christmas without your husband, or how you're going to clean the air conditioning ducts. It's not the decision itself that's so hard; it's the fact that it reminds you that you're alone, and that your dear husband is not there to make it with you. No matter how long-lasting his illness, and no matter how many times you rehearsed what you'd do when that terrible moment came—inevitably, you weren't ready. Oh, you carried out your duties perfectly, but inside, you were yelling, "Wait! I'm not ready!"

Perhaps six months will go by, and you'll still be saying, "I'm not ready." Let's face it; we never want to be without our loved ones. Coming to terms with widowhood is no easy task. You may experience a strange, soupy sensation in your head; you can't focus and you don't want to. Finding yourself a widow feels like suddenly realizing that part of your limbs are missing. You might discover yourself looking over your shoulder, trying to catch a glimpse of your husband—before you remember he's no longer with you. It's a shock, and it happens over and over. You wonder, where is he? Then it hits you: he's *gone.*

There is an odd disorientation in finding yourself alone this way. It's not like being at home when your husband was traveling for business or visiting relatives—some of us used that time, gratefully, to catch up on things (especially if we too had a job). This is different; there's nothing to catch up on, you think, because everything's *over*. At least that's how you may feel at first. You wander around the house, wondering what to do—or you have to get out of the house; you can't stay there, because it's so empty. Maybe you find yourself unable to *think* in your home—that's quite common. You begin to do something, forget what you're doing, and start crying in frustration. Maybe your ears are ringing, and you can't seem to stop it.

It's called grief. All of it: the physical as well as the emotional symptoms.

And not only do you have your own emotions to deal with, you have the feelings of others: your spouse's brothers, sisters, cousins, and your children; whether all together or separately you have to deal with their grief as well. You may even have his parents to consider if they are alive, or yours. Often you may find yourself, in the first few months, putting your own feelings aside to be dealt with later, while you comfort some of those relatives who may have been taken by surprise. Perform this service gladly—it will fit in with one of the above-mentioned rules, which I'm going to talk about further: "do something nice for someone else."

But don't worry—you'll have plenty of support for yourself. People are extremely nice to widows, maybe because they know it's part of the romantic mystery of life and love. And if you don't get enough comforting, this book will help you learn how to comfort yourself, perhaps in ways you've never dreamed of.

So take a deep breath, dear widow, and prepare yourself for a journey such as you've never known before. The journey will take you through all the stages of your love for your husband, and beyond. Ultimately, your voyage will lead you to your deepest self, the self you know best, but have perhaps forgotten in your grief.

Guidelnes for Learning to Live Alone as a Widow

1. Get out of bed every day, wash your face and eat something. Even if you spend the day in bed (and that's okay, as long as you don't do it regularly), you will have gotten up and greeted the morning—very important!

2. Make a list at the beginning of the week of everything you'd like to accomplish, Monday through Friday. You can have the weekend off.

3. Do at least three-fourths of what's on that list.

4. Make sure you have unlimited phone time, if you can afford it. Friends and relatives should be available to you at all hours, for as long as you want. (This is so important you can even substitute it for a vacation. You may not feel like traveling extensively anyhow.)

5. Eat dinner. If you don't like to cook, get take-out, go out with a friend or buy a barbecued chicken at the grocery store. Don't deprive yourself of food.

6. On the other hand, don't gorge. If you have a tendency to turn to food for solace, get that under control as soon as possible, with Lean Cuisine, salads or the Leave 1/3 Diet (more on that later). A lot of what you're going through has to do with self-esteem—getting fat won't do much for how you view yourself.

7. Go out and buy something nice for yourself the first week of your widowhood. It could be a new lamp, a bottle of perfume, or a new pair of pajamas—something that brings you comfort. If you don't have much money, indulge in some scented body lotion, a bouquet of flowers or a writing journal with a pretty cover. (These can be had for as little as $8 at your nearby Barnes & Noble. You're going to need one eventually—might as well get it now.)

8. Establish some schedules with your friends. Maybe one of your single women friends is available on Saturday

nights: go to the movies or out to dinner with her. A working friend with many responsibilities may only be available on Friday afternoons for lunch; a busy retired woman who volunteers at numerous organizations may be available on Tuesdays and Thursdays. All your friends will want to see you, and you can usually arrange something on an on-going basis with your closest pals. You don't have to occupy yourself with friends every day of the week—but establishing some sort of routine will ease your anxiety about being alone so much so *suddenly*. (After all, you and your husband probably had a little routine for going out—you're used to that.)

9. Make your bed and wash the dishes every day. (All right, we said you could have occasional days spent in bed. You don't have to make your bed that day.)

10. Do nice things for yourself as often as possible. It doesn't have to be much. It can be stopping by a park on the way home from the grocery store and looking at the trees. It can be wearing a favorite piece of jewelry for no particular reason. You can go to Starbucks for a café mocha (or get one at McDonald's); take a bubble bath in the middle of the day; go swimming at your neighborhood pool. You can stay up late and watch an old sitcom on TV, or spend a couple of hours looking up frivolous information on the Internet—like vacation homes in Tuscany, or bios of movie stars—things you normally wouldn't take the time to do. You can buy yourself a new lipstick before the old one is used up, or treat yourself to an apple turnover for breakfast. But whatever you do, don't feel guilty doing it. Remember, your husband would not want you to be miserable. You owe it to him to take care of yourself.

Chapter Two

Two Rules for Survival

There is married, and there is *married*. Most of my friends, influenced by the women's empowerment movement of the 1970s, worked at jobs they liked, even if they had children. They had careers, meaning their job wasn't just something to do for money—it was meaningful work that fulfilled a part of their being. These women weren't married in the same way their mothers were married. No matter how much they loved their husbands, from the very beginning of their adult lives they sought satisfaction through paths *in addition* to marriage.

If you were one of these women, be grateful. Be grateful that you learned early on that your whole meaning in life does not rest solely with a man. If you were not one of these women, be grateful too, because you're going to learn this valuable truth now. And these are just two of the many blessings you should be grateful for. Cultivating gratitude is one of the cardinal rules for getting through the first six to eight months of widowhood.

"What!" you cry, "I should be grateful that my husband died?"

No, that's not what your gratitude is for. Your gratitude—and you should start exercising it early, as soon as possible after the memorial service—your gratitude is for the fact that you had a husband for as many years as you did. For five years, or 10 years, 15 or 35—you had a person to think about, care for, worry about, plan with, pamper, have sex with, go places with, and celebrate with. You had a husband. Be grateful.

There are many ways to express gratitude for your husband. One of the first things I learned from my friend Marie, a wise woman who has been a widow for many years, is to bless other couples whenever you see them. This may seem hard. There you are, *hurting*, and you're supposed to feel good about seeing couples holding hands? No, you don't necessarily have to feel good about this, at first (but you soon will). Think about it: there are couples everywhere, and you are a new widow—you're going to notice them. What are you going to do, silently hope they'll fall on their noses as they walk arm in arm though the park? No! You bless them—it doesn't have to be very elaborate; just say those two words: bless you. This is part of gratitude, and of you being grateful for all the years you were a couple. Within one or two weeks it will be a welcome task.

There are many other ways to express gratitude for the years you spent with your husband. You can look at photographs of yourselves together, talk about your loved one with dear and trusted friends (be *sure* to do this—it's part of the healing process). You can visit places you used to go together, taking a friend along (more on this later). You can start making lists of all your blessings. (I suggest starting this within the first month—don't be surprised if it brings tears of gratitude to your eyes.) As time progresses, your list will begin to encompass other things in your life: the new iphone you got for yourself, and the exercise regime you've successfully undertaken. But, if you're lucky, you'll carry that gratitude you felt for the years you spent with your husband with you. It's like food: it will nourish you, and help you grow.

The second rule for survival is: Do something nice for someone else. I remembered this from hard times past (my parents both died when I was barely 40), and was able to put it into effect almost immediately. A few days after the memorial services, I went back to the funeral home to collect some things—photos used in the DVD, and some memorabilia that had been displayed. The funeral director, Michelle, was very kind and spent a long time talking with me about grieving—she'd lost her sister the year before. I felt comfortable with her, especially when she told me she was a writer and had written several plays. One of them, it turned out, had been produced at a venue in Orlando. Suddenly, half remembering my second rule for survival, I blurted out, "The college where I've been teaching has a performing arts center. Would you like me to see if we could put your play on there?"

Michelle's eyes lit up, as much, I think, by my use of the word "we" as the suggestion of a prestigious venue for her play. "Oh, wow, that would be fan-*tas*-tic!" she said, clasping my hand. "Do you really think it's possible?"

I didn't know; I'd retired from teaching a year ago to take care of my husband, but I'd kept my ties with the college and something told me to go ahead—if nothing else, I was expressing my support of Michelle's play, and maybe, at the moment, that's what *she* needed.

During the following week, in between dealing with banks and hospital bills, I made a phone call to another teacher at the college, Helen, who was one of my good friends. Helen suggested bringing Michelle to a meeting of the Women's Conference Committee; the play could be presented without cost if it had the sponsorship of a college organization. Serendipitously, the Conference Committee was meeting the following Wednesday. Helen said she'd make sure that Michelle and I were on the agenda.

The next week, Michelle presented a spellbinding synopsis of her play, and the group gave her a round of applause when she was through, and agreed immediately to sponsor the production. I didn't have to say a word. Yet I knew that this act of encouraging and supporting another human being, no matter how small, had already been a big step in my healing. I had made an effort to get outside of myself by turning my eyes back toward the world, instead of focusing only on my inner world of grief. I'm not saying you shouldn't grieve the loss of your husband, but a balance needs to be established as early as possible between you and the outside world. In the beginning of your widowhood, that balance will be teetering precariously inward, so that you are overly conscious of your every thought and feeling, the noises in your house, even your own heartbeats. But the human mind can only focus on one thing at a time—as you direct your thoughts to someone else's needs, you tip the balance back to equilibrium. And that's what you need—to regain your balance.

There was one other benefit to getting involved in Michelle's play. The Women's Conference Committee at the college had meetings every other week. Michelle, dressed in business attire for her job as Funeral Director, met me outside the building, and we'd go in together. So naturally, I began dressing up too: suits, scarves, jewelry.

There's nothing like pretty clothes for restoring some women's confidence, and I am one of those women. Maybe you are, too.

Guidelines: Two Rules for Survival

Gratitude

1. When you get up in the morning, express gratitude that you had your husband as long as you did. You can do this by writing down some thoughts in a journal, saying a prayer, or just thinking grateful thoughts.

2. Talk about your loved one with friends, mentioning particularly nice things your husband did for you and others.

3. Make a list of everything that you have to be grateful for. Post the list in a conspicuous place: near your computer, on the refrigerator, or in a journal you use every day.

4. Take yourself out to lunch at a favorite place, and feel grateful to be lunching there. Savor the food; admire the ambiance.

5. Go to a movie that you know will touch you. Be grateful that you can still be touched.

Do Something for Someone Else

1. Buy a little gift for one of your husband's relatives. Sisters, brothers, even cousins may be hurting as much as you are—making this effort will help you both.

2. Invite a friend or neighbor who was especially helpful to you during your husband's last year out to lunch or dinner, or ask if there's anything you can do for that person.

3. Select a charity and donate some of your husband's best clothes to that cause. I chose AmVets, since my husband was a veteran. (No, you probably can't do this right away, and you may want to tackle it in several steps, but you'll be amazed at how comforting it is to imagine your husband's clothes put to a very special use.)

4. Volunteer your services at a local organization, even if only for a short time. I offered to write press releases for a local museum; organizations like Hospice always need help. You don't have to commit yourself for the rest of your life; the rule of thumb for widowhood is, don't make any major decisions the first year. Just help

out a little, when you're ready and for as long as you like.

5. Open yourself to unexpected opportunities to help people, such as my encounter with Michelle. When you are available to help others, opportunities will present themselves.

Chapter Three

Nurturing Yourself

Grieving effectively is about finding a balance between two worlds. On the one hand, there is the life you had with your husband; you miss it, and him; you wish he were still with you. Often there is pain involved in your memories. On the other hand, you know you have to go on—there are a million details to take care of in connection with his passing, your current job (if you have one, or maybe now you have to *find* one). Your children, other relatives, friends and other individuals in your life will expect you to carry on. No one wants you to go to pieces—and you don't really want to either, do you?

One of the best ways to handle both the emotions and the sense of unreality that grieving brings, along with the responsibilities of carrying on, is to nurture yourself. Get in the habit of this, early and often—from day one of your mourning. The idea is to treat yourself the way you'd like some loving person—a mother, sister, or friend—to care for you, if you could tell them exactly what you needed.

"That's all very well," you say helplessly, "but I don't really know exactly what I need. My feelings are confused."

Of course they are. You've been through a trauma. All the more reason why you need "special handling." How can we figure out what will really soothe us, and what will provide some comfort for that ongoing pain inside? My friend Beth (not a widow) taught me to make a list of "Nice Things to Do." This list will probably change a bit every week—just like you'll change every week. Yet several of your favorite items will always be on your list. (Check out some of my "Nice Things to Do" lists in the Appendix.)

I first learned about nurturing myself after my father died when I was 39 years old. I was living on the North Shore of Long Island, having moved out of Manhattan with my second husband. He had a job out there; I had—grief. I mourned my father continually but didn't know what to do about it. Finally, I sought a therapist, who told me I was depressed. Among other remedies, he suggested I go shopping.

"Go shopping?" I asked. "How on earth will that help?"

My therapist assured me it would. So, shopping I went, making myself buy one item on every excursion, no matter how "down" I felt. I bought pretty soap, costume jewelry, and small, unusual handbags. Later, more impulsively, I bought gypsy skirts, peasant blouses, and a wonderful blue and rose fringed shawl. I also bought things for my husband, but the therapist said that didn't count: I was trying to nurture *me*.

Sometime later, after several months of nurturing, during which my depression began to lift, I was heading out for a shopping trip when I realized, in a burst of insight, that I had become my own mother. (My mother, although helpful, was 1000 miles away, and dealing with her own grief.) Nurturing that little rascal, "the inner child," I had assumed a parent role, taking care of the needy self who'd been so terribly depressed. As a loving "parent," I knew exactly what that child within needed—and I was happy to give it to her. She needed love, symbolized by the act of giving something, no matter how tedious or hopeless it might appear. She needed beauty, because beauty has a way of soothing the depressed soul— the beauty of color, design and fabric, as found in clothes, for instance. And as time went on, I found other ways to nurture myself besides shopping: visits to art galleries and museums, long drives to scenic locales, and solo lunches of pasta primavera or salad Nicoise—not expensive, but colorful.

The secret of self-nurturing, which is essential for success, is that you must do it alone. If you go shopping with a friend, no matter how sympathetic that person is, your attention will be on that individual and not on yourself. Remember, you are acting as your *own* mother here—not your friend's. Now that I've had the opportunity to see how effective nurturing is, I am a confirmed champion of the solo lunch, where you choose a lovely bistro overlooking the park, or perhaps in the heart of the city with a cozy fireplace in the background. I love the solitary visit to a museum or gallery, a movie or planetarium. Everything you indulge in with your inner child will pay you rewards (and remember, as a widow, you can go anywhere alone, without feeling out of place).

This step is so important in your grieving process that I propose you start it the week after your husband's memorial service. You don't have to tell anyone—just go shopping!

Guidelines for Nurturing Yourself

1. As soon as you are able, make a list of "Nice Things to Do." The list should include activities such as lunches out at favorite places, purchases you'd like to make (no matter how small—I usually put "buy blue pens" on my list), and places you'd like to visit. Try to do one or two items on your list each week.

2. Look through the myriad of catalogues that arrive at your house, or go online—and order something.

3. Take a drive on a nice day—with or without a destination.

4. Go to a beach, a park, or a museum, and mindlessly enjoy it.

5. See a movie once a week—more if you can afford it.

6. Do something impractical that you've wanted to do for a long time. Take a jewelry making class or hula lessons, or go fly-fishing. (Eeek!)

7. Make some favorite foods that you haven't prepared in a long time—chicken cordon bleu, banana cream pie, New England clam chowder, or cheese grits. Something yummy and delicious, but not impossible to make. Enjoy this favorite food with a glass of wine, iced tea or lemonade.

8. Make a reservation at a hotel or motel in a nearby city (or your own city or town). Don't worry whether you will actually keep your reservation—the act of making it is nurturing in itself.

9. Go there!

10. Order room service.

Chapter Four

Make a Plan

While it's good to drift awhile after the memorial service and to let yourself be taken care of, if possible, by relatives and friends, within a few weeks you will probably be wise to make yourself a little plan. This is not something to worry about; just make some notes when you're relatively relaxed—after a hot bath, for example, or maybe during a coffee break if you're working. You can jot down the basics of your plan on a napkin, if necessary, and then transfer it to your journal or computer.

Your plan should cover four basic areas (you can modify these to suit your own needs):

1. Things to take care of now (in one to three months)
2. Things to take care of soon (in three to six months)
3. Items to be tabled until a later date
4. Your desires

Now, I know Item #4 doesn't seem to fit the seriousness of the first three, but actually, "Your desires" are the most important element of your plan. "Your desires" are *you*, and what you want to do. Items 1, 2 and 3—let's face it—are probably things you don't want to do, but have to do anyway. So, let's get started:

Things to take care of now (in one to three months)

1. We're assuming you have gone through the funeral and/or memorial service, and paid for all the expenses involved. If you haven't paid for everything or made payment arrangements, this would be the first thing to take care of on your list.

2. Probate. If your house, bank accounts, business or any other property or possessions were in your husband's name and not yours, you will have to go through probate. This means seeing a lawyer. I was fortunate, because two days before my husband died, he put my name on all his bank accounts, including his business accounts. My name was already on the deed to our house; in some states, the wife automatically retains ownership of the house, even if her name is not on the deed. Note: Be very careful about approaching the bank if you have a mortgage with your husband's name on it. I've heard some horror stories about inflated interest rates due to a difference in credit reports—this might be the time to talk to a lawyer. Most states have legal aid groups available to help widows if you can't afford to hire an attorney.

3. Hospital bills. You may not have these, but if you do, you will want to take care of them right away. Often payment arrangements can be made for extensive hospital bills; be prepared to talk to the hospital right away. (You will hear from them *soon*.)

4. Social Security. You don't really have to take care of this right away, but if you need to, go ahead and make the call. Social Security has some very nice people in their bereavement department who will help you transfer your husband's social security to your account (you are entitled to one, not both). You will also be signed up for widow's benefits if you qualify. Call the main number, in the middle of the week, about 11 a.m., and you'll get to talk to somebody.

5. Make a list of all the personal things, particular to you that you need to take care of now and/or in the near future. My list included such items as, cleaning out my

husband's business building, paying his sales tax, and selling his film and video editing equipment. No, you don't have to *do* all these things now—just make a list.

Things to take care of soon (in three to six months)

The shock is starting to subside, but guilt and memories may be taking its place, so don't be surprised if this is an unexpectedly hard period for getting things done. Here's what you can try:

1. Start clearing your husband's closets. Now, I'm not saying you *must* do this—but if you can, even a tiny bit, you will feel better about yourself. The closet is one of the hardest things to tackle. I suggest picking a favorite charity and selecting some of your husband's best items of clothing to donate. This way you'll know you're really helping someone in your grief.

2. Make your own will and funeral arrangements if you haven't done so. Again, this is one of those tasks that, while difficult under the circumstances, will make you feel better after you've accomplished it—more grounded, more secure.

3. Start sorting through your husband's bills and papers. If you are not in probate, you may have to take care of a few of these during this period. Do so, but treat yourself well after each effort. I went out and bought a bottle of perfume after closing my husband's bank accounts, because it was hard!

4. Assess your own financial situation. You may have done this earlier of course, depending on what shape your finances are in. But—here's the key—assess only. Don't do anything drastic, like sell your stocks or put your house on the market. It's still way too soon. Again, remember the widow's rule of thumb: don't make any major decisions the first year. (However, if you need to get a job, it's okay to start thinking about it.)

5. Plan a little vacation. At the end of six months, see if you can treat yourself to a little trip. It doesn't have to be far—maybe visit a friend in another state. Or just go to a nearby city and stay in a hotel for a few days. You deserve it.

Items to be tabled until a later date

1. Cleaning out any icky, messy anything! Let's face it, there are some things you just don't want to do. You'd be happy if you never had to do it, but you certainly don't want to do it *now*. Don't. There is no rule that says everything has to get taken care of in the first six months—or even during the first year. If there's some onerous task you know you have to do, but you just can't face it—put it off for a while, please.

   For me, it was cleaning out my husband's business building. This was a two-story house on the main thoroughfare of town, crammed to the gills with video equipment, film equipment, DVDs, CDs, VHS tapes (you can see how long this stuff had accumulated), invoices, film cans, papers, magazines and much, much more. This building, in fact, contained some 30-odd years of my husband's video and film editing business—he'd moved his New York office down to Florida in 2008. Two floors—and it was my job to sort it all out. I decided that when the time came and I was ready, I'd hire people to help me. I'd be less likely to get emotional, I thought, if surrounded by strangers. When I was ready, I'd tackle that building—and not a moment before.

   If you have a project like this—a work shed, a storage unit, or a home office that you just can't face right now, table it until a later date. After all, it's not going anywhere, is it?

2. I'm going to put cleaning out hubby's closets and drawers in this section too, because for some people,

that is an unbearable task. I cleaned out some drawers, some closets, and tabled others. There's no rush, honey. (Don't worry what the neighbors, your relatives or friends will think. This is your life, and your healing—not theirs.)

3. Selling his car. Like clothes and business equipment, getting rid of your husband's car may cause you some heartache. Let it wait—unless you really need the money a possible sale will bring. Having hubby's car in the garage a while longer may prove soothing.

4. Selling your house. Some widows want to move right away, and others don't. Again, remember the widow's rule. My friend Anne was faced with a new house when her husband unexpectedly passed away, but she wisely waited a couple of years before putting it on the market. In the meantime, she invited a friend to rent a room, thus helping with expenses and providing some company as well.

Your Desires

Of all the categories, this will probably be the hardest to fill out on your plan. Plan that trip to Hawaii you've always wanted to take, or go back to school to get a Master's degree. This is your private list that tells you: yes, you are still alive, and you still have plans for your life. Your husband would have wanted you to have such plans—he certainly would not have wanted you to quit living. Don't worry if you can't get into this list right away. Desires can be hard things to come by, and sometimes the thing to do is to let them find you.

Maybe you'll drive by the local community college and remember you've always wanted to take a photography class: make a note of it. If a television ad shows a new car with a great warranty, and you're interested: make a note of it. If your sister calls and suggests a trip to Ireland, and you're in no mood to go now but you'd like to visit someday: make a note of it. Eventually, all these notes will form a list of things you'd like to do—maybe not now, but in the future. You have desires. You're alive. Your husband would have wanted it that way.

Guildelines for Making a Plan

1. Wait until you're feeling a little bit cheerful to start making your plan—maybe when someone's done something nice for you, or you've received an especially heart-warming note of condolence. Making a plan can be hard, so you want to be as upbeat as possible (and I know that's not easy right now).

2. Don't do the whole plan in one sitting. As suggested, let ideas come to you while you're at dinner, or out shopping. The "your desires" part in particular, should not be rushed.

3. Be as detailed as possible about each item on your plan—including phone numbers, email addresses and other important data.

4. As you complete each item, cross it off your list.

5. Make another list of the items you've accomplished each month.

6. Take your plan, and make a weekly schedule of the things you must do, and try to stick to it. This is particularly good if your emotions are all over the place—having a list can ground you. (More later on making lists.)

7. If you can't seem to accomplish a particular item the first three months, move it to the 3-6 month plan.

8. If you still can't do this item, move it to the "tabled" department.

9. Don't beat yourself up for not doing things—reward yourself for accomplishing them.

10. Congratulate yourself for having a plan.

Chapter Five

Tears

Your husband has been gone about a month, maybe two, and you're still crying every day. Oh, not all day, and not un-controllable bawling—but yes, you're shedding tears. Is this normal, you ask? How long will it go on?

Buck up, girl. You may find yourself crying in some form for six or seven months, maybe more. But the type of tears you shed may change—going from bouts of heart-broken sobbing to a moistening of the eye and a tug of the heart when you see or hear something that reminds you of your husband. There's nothing wrong with this—in fact, it's better to cry than to bottle up your emotions.

I was one of those stoic widows at my husband's memorial service. The image of a dry-eyed Jackie Kennedy firmly implanted in my mind, I went through all the public ceremonies without a tear. Only when I was alone did I let myself go—and then I cried my eyes out.

But because I was with family and friends those first few weeks, the free-flow of tears didn't happen too much. My brother Robert came to stay with me for two weeks right after Jack's passing, and he cheered me up considerably. I was often with friends and neighbors during that period as well, which lifted my spirits. When Robert went home to San Diego, I was more lonesome than ever and knew I had to do something—fast. So I booked a two-night stay at the Marriott in Key Largo. Yes, it was a splurge, but as we've discussed in "Nurturing Yourself," splurges and treats are the best way to deal with your pain right now.

And so, on a brilliant Saturday morning in mid-January, I set off for Key Largo in my little Hyundai, armed with a box of Krispy Kreme glazed donuts. I also had some gospel music CDs, and put one on as soon as I got on I-95, knowing it was exactly what I needed to hear. I drove straight through from Daytona to Key Largo, some 275 miles, with just one pit stop. On the way, I had a moment of healing.

I'd been on the road about 20 minutes, munching on do-nuts and listening to the gospel music. I started singing along with one of the songs—and as I did the tears began to flow. For some 200 miles I sang and cried and drove. Something was happening in me—a cleansing of pain, a washing away of agony through my tears. I was reaching out—through travel, through music, through the beautiful day—to the hope that I somehow knew awaited me on the other side of my tears.

So, I cried, not non-stop, but on and off the whole way to Key Largo. My singing brought me closer to love: love for my husband, for myself, and for God who was taking care of me. My tears brought a relief from pain—the tears merged with the love into a comforting melee of emotion. It's true, some-times, that we can't tell pain from love when it's very intense.

When I finally reached Key Largo, I was shaking with the feeling of re-birth and love for my husband—and also a new and wondrous understanding of death. I'm sure Jackie Ken-nedy cried after her husband's death; she just did it alone, in her own way, and in her own time.

That's what you've got to do: cry. Let your tears wash away the pain you're feeling—don't bottle it up. If you find yourself getting weepy during a drive to the country, a televi-sion movie, even a commercial—let it come. If you're cry-ing on the inside, why not let it out? Be kind to yourself—cry, baby, cry. It's good for you, and even if it continues for months—so what? Eventually you'll ease up, though you may not stop crying completely for some time.

Why should you? You loved him. (Hey, I'm getting a few tears just writing this!) Love, emotions, and feelings—these are the most powerful sensations in the world, and often, they are accompanied by *tears*.

Guidelines for Dealing with Tears

1. If you find yourself crying unexpectedly as you watch TV or read a book, put the book down, and let the tears come. They will help you heal.

2. Find some "alone" time so that you can release your tears, unimpeded. Do this as often as necessary.

3. If you find yourself getting tearful while talking to a friend, explain what's going on. Believe me, everyone will understand.

4. Try not to be embarrassed by your tears, or any of your emotions. You've got enough to think about right now without worrying over "appearances."

5. As time goes on, you may notice more of your tears are related to happy memories. This is a good sign—the pain is changing into unadulterated love.

Chapter Six

Friends

When you're hit by a shock, such as you might be feeling after your husband's death, the tendency may be to bury yourself in your house and lick your wounds. While alone time is certainly necessary, the value of friends and relatives in your recovery process cannot be measured.

One of the first things I did to reach out to friends and relatives was mail copies of Jack's obituary notice, along with a little note, to people in different cities who might not have heard about his passing. You can send these notes via email with an attachment, of course, but I got more out of writing a personal note. This is as much for you as for the person you're sending it to—also, I remember that Jack had once received such a note from the wife of an old friend who'd passed on, and he was sincerely touched.

In your note, mention how much your husband valued that friend or relative. For instance, in writing to old friends who worked on a movie Jack and I had produced, I might say, "Jack always thought so highly of your professional abilities, and was so grateful for your help on our film." Be absolutely sincere in everything you say—this is not the time for exaggeration. You will probably find yourself overwhelmed with love for the person as you write—and it is, figuratively, a way for you to put yourself in your husband's shoes for a brief time, and to think with his thoughts.

You might not be able to write more than one of these notes a day. I was still sending them out two months after Jack's passing, but it was one of the most rewarding tasks I did—not only the writing of the notes, but the receipt of condolence letters in return.

Another important function of friends is to buffer your re-entry into the world. You may notice, as you travel around town, that certain places you frequented with your husband have now become NO-FLY zones—that is, you don't want to go there. Friends can help you deal with this.

Caribbean Jack's was a favorite spot where my husband and I went on Friday nights or Sunday afternoons to hear music. The crowd was especially mellow on Sundays, and Jack loved to watch the boats pulling into the marina as the sunset settled around us. After a couple of months, I noticed I was avoiding the street where this establishment was located—even though it was near my home. One Sunday I'd been having dinner with my friend Helen, and as we drove home, impulsively I asked her to join me for a drink at Caribbean Jack's.

"I've got to break the stigma of this place," I told her. "Will you come with me?"

"Of course," she said immediately, pulling into the parking lot. We made our way out to the deck, where Jack and I had always settled, and ordered a drink. When the drinks arrived, Helen clinked glasses with me. "To Jack," she said, smiling. A shiver went through me, but I was okay, and profoundly grateful to her for breaking the taboo of the place for me.

A week later, another pal, Carole, invited me to spend the weekend with her. I was nervous about my "new" widow hours—I tended to stay up very late now, often reading till I fell asleep at 3 a.m., or sometimes waking at 4 a.m. and roaming the house. How would I deal with that at Carole's house?

I didn't have to. My dear friend made me a scrumptious dinner, complete with apple pie and ice cream. After dinner, we watched the movie "Dragonfly" together. I was riveted: the film was about a scientist, played by Kevin Costner, whose wife is killed and revisits him in the form of a dragonfly—or so we are led to believe. Whether it was the movie, or Carole's apple pie, I slept like a baby that night, and the rest of the weekend was a joy.

Friends can do more than just provide comfort. They can give you a lifeline back to the world of work. About two months after Jack passed away, a dear friend, Karen, asked me to edit a book she was writing. The manuscript, already formatted since she was publishing it independently, concerned Karen's spiritual journey—a compelling, well documented voyage of discovery through all four corners of the world. I began work about a month later, and found myself completely caught up in the project. (It didn't hurt that Karen paid for my services either.) Scheduling a regular work time each day to edit the book provided me with a structure, something that is definitely needed while coping with the insecurity of widowhood. Plus, as the book became more involving, I found I was lifted out of myself and my concerns, and forced to focus my attention on the editing problems at hand. The work took on a life of its own.

There will come a time—maybe six months down the road of your widowhood, maybe longer, when you will need to make a leap. You'll say, "I'm ready to re-enter the world"--but you may need what amounts to a rite of passage to accomplish this. Once again, look to your friends to help you navigate this rite. I had been working on Karen's book for two months, and my job there was almost through: in another two weeks, I'd be returning to a part-time teaching job: faculty meetings, syllabi, and of course, eager and demanding students. Was I ready for this? Was I ready to re-enter the work-world—or was I still a grieving widow?

An old pal, Diane, offered me the opportunity to find out, inviting me up to her house in the North Carolina mountains, some 500 miles away. On the way I planned to stop in Atlanta to pick up Cheryl, another long-time friend, and the three of us, who hadn't been together in over five years, would celebrate a lovely, overdue reunion.

Once again, I was nervous. Could I safely drive alone through Atlanta traffic, find my way to Cheryl's house, and make it up to North Carolina in my now five-year old car? Normally I'd have welcomed the travel, but in my grieving state, I found myself imagining troubling scenarios. What if the car broke down on the highway, and I had to call AAA while Cheryl broiled in the forecasted 100 degree weather? What if we broke down somewhere that cell phone service wasn't even available?

I serviced my car as well as I was able, buying a new tire at the last minute when my mechanic showed me some bubbles on one of the old ones. That might have caused some problems, so I was grateful for his calling attention to the situation. God was definitely in charge.

As it turned out, I had no car difficulties, and everything went as planned. I picked up Cheryl, stayed overnight at her house in Atlanta and visited the dance class she taught the following day. We then travelled up to Ashville to picnic in the Blue Ridge Mountains, sightsee, shop and even participate in a wild night of hippie drumming that Ashville is famous for. The last night of our visit, Diane hosted a cookout for her women's group; sitting around a bonfire, women talked about their husbands, and I realized, with a shock, that I no longer had one. When one of the gals read a poem she'd written about her spouse, I unexpectedly choked up—

it was all too much. The mountains, the drumming, and the poetry—I missed Jack!

And so I talked about it—with Diane, with Cheryl, and with six other women I'd just met, as we drank Sangria, ate homegrown corn and broiled hot dogs over a campfire. Cathartic? You bet!

Friends will help you ease your transition from death to life—if you are willing to let them get close to you.

Guidelines for Friends

1. Be very, very grateful for your friends and relatives.

2. Be open and honest about your feelings of loss—this is no place for stoicism.

3. If you are with a friend and suddenly feel emotional about your husband's death—discuss it. The emotion means you are with a friend who cares.

4. Accept all invitations to go out with friends and relatives, even if you don't feel like it.

5. Make extra effort with friends. If someone invites you to lunch, or to spend the weekend, be sure to follow up with a thank you of some kind. It's possible your friend has made a real effort on your behalf.

6. Guard against withdrawing from friends and relatives as you come out of the fog of widowhood. Yes, you feel better—but your friend will worry if you suddenly stop returning phone calls.

7. Remember that long discussions of your widowhood, your trials and tribulations may make some people feel uncomfortable—especially those married friends whose husbands may not be doing too well healthwise.

8. Watch out for needy friends, who may use your widowhood as an opportunity to latch onto you more

than you'd really like. Strong as you may feel at times, you're still in need of support yourself—don't become a "sponge" for others' complaints.

9. Allow your friends to lead you to the next level—a wise and loving friend can sometimes discern exactly what you need, whether it's a night out with the girls, a weekend away, or a new job opportunity.

10. Be patient with friends—remember, until you yourself are a widow, you cannot know what it's like. Sometimes, even with the best of intentions, a friend will say something that hurts you. That person probably didn't mean to. Forgive and forget!

Chapter Seven

Cooking for One

One of the most daunting situations to face as a new widow is the prospect of eating alone. It's right up there with handling holidays, except the tears you'll shed, if any, will probably be tears of frustration rather than grief. Dinnertime will creep up on you, and you'll find you're not prepared. Shaking your head in irritation, you'll head out—again—to the Boston Market, or the takeout Chinese, or maybe Sonny's Bar-B-Q drive-through window. After all, you want to eat, and you want something good.

Many widows handle the problem by going out to eat every night with friends. Celeste, who has been widowed for two years, told me that, after her husband died, she promised herself she'd never cook again. If you can afford to go out to dinner every night, and that's your preference, by all means do so. At least you'll probably get a serving of all the basic food groups, and you won't have to do any dishes. I love to go out and try to dine with friends at least two or three times a week, although sometimes these meals are pretty casual.

If your budget doesn't allow a nightly visit to a nice restaurant, and you're starting to get tired of take-out chicken or pulled pork sandwiches, it's time to walk back into the kitchen and take a look around. Yes, it's true: many single people never cook—when they find themselves alone at home during dinnertime, they open a can of something or stick something into the microwave and eat standing at the kitchen sink.

The problem is, as a married woman, you're probably used to having a real dinner. So here you are, a new widow, already hurting from your loss—are you going to endure further punishment by depriving yourself of a good meal at the end of the day? You know how to cook—but you're uncomfortable fixing dinner for just one person. Is it really worth all the fuss and bother to cook for just you?

The answer is—yes. Not only is it worth it, cooking a nice dinner for yourself is a way to give yourself love and nurturing, ingredients so very important as you heal from the loss of your husband. So put on that apron, dear widow and get back into your groove, cooking-wise.

I had not done a lot of cooking in recent years, although at earlier periods of my life I'd been pretty proficient in the kitchen. Jack loved to cook, and as his health deteriorated and he spent more and more time at home, he began to watch cooking shows—Rachel Ray, the Barefoot Contessa, Julia Child reruns, and all the other numerous chefs on the cooking network. The result was some pretty fantastic dinners—blackened fish with five spices and fresh mint topped with a lemon/lime sauce; boeuf bourguignonne; steamed sea scallops with vegetables, split pea soup with cinnamon, and many other tasty treats. I got spoiled. However, after a few weeks I'd discovered that all Jack's spices were still in the kitchen, and even though he never used recipes, he always told me how he'd created his dishes. I didn't attempt anything very fancy at first, but I felt my husband's love in the kitchen, which made it comfortable to cook there.

In the very early days after his passing, right after my brother left, I indulged myself with some of the prepared selections in the meat counter at the grocery store. The flank steak wrapped around mozzarella was good, and all you had to do was heat it in the oven for about 40 minutes. With it, I'd have broccoli or green beans (frozen is easy and quick) and fresh bread and butter. Voila, a home-cooked meal, which I served to myself on a tray with a glass of wine, and ate while watching something good on TV. Other tasty selections from the prepared food corner included meatloaf, pork tenderloin and chicken Florentine. After a while I graduated to the seafood counter, to salmon pinwheels stuffed with crabmeat—absolutely delicious, but since they're not pre-packaged there are no instructions for cooking, so you have to keep an eye on them. Frozen peas or spinach make a good accompaniment, and you might try the stuffed tilapia for a variation.

As I became more comfortable, I made spaghetti and meatballs, feeling the spirit of my husband, who was half Italian, hovering over me when I cooked. "Don't overcook the sauce," he'd caution—or was that my own inner chef advising me? On light days, I'd settle for a Swiss cheese omelet made with Jarlsberg, along with toast—but always attractively served on a tray with knife, fork, napkin, and a small glass of wine to add a festive touch.

When the weather warmed, I began to make huge salads for lunch: romaine lettuce, with tomatoes, hard boiled eggs, or shredded chicken if I'd made broiled chicken the night before. The dressing was always olive oil (I discovered a huge 3-liter jug of olive oil in the pantry, compliments of Jack), with balsamic vinegar and fresh garlic, and salt and pepper. With the advent of the salad, I was now making all three meals for myself (breakfast, I confess, was usually yogurt and toast), and I began to feel like I was really taking care of myself. I cut out the wine for a while, and lost a little weight—mostly the extra pounds I'd put on in the first month as I gorged while dining out with my brother.

But, frankly, it's not the health aspects that are so beneficial in going into the kitchen and cooking dinner for yourself. It's the fact that you've cared enough about *you* to prepare a nice meal—even though you're only cooking for one.

GUIDLELINES FOR COOKING FOR ONE

1. Don't cut yourself off from having a good dinner every day—you have enough to struggle through without being mean to yourself at night.

2. Any time you even think of cooking, walk into your kitchen and take a look around. Assemble some ingredients for whatever you've been thinking of making—even if you don't make it, you will have broken the "cooking for one" disinclination.

3. Start with easy things, such as those prepared items at the end of the meat counter that just need heating in the oven: stuffed pork chops, meat loaf, or chicken breasts with spinach. These entrees are often very good and will get you to make the connection between putting something in the oven and eating a good meal.

4. After you've broken the ice, try making something that you always cooked easily before, such as omelets or spaghetti. Cooking is rather like sex or riding a bicycle; it'll all come back to you once you get in the saddle.

5. Serve yourself nicely. No standing at the kitchen sink and wolfing down a meal. Put your plate on a tray with a knife and fork, or seat yourself at a table. Yes, a book or TV accompaniment is fine—we're trying to relax here, not prove something to somebody!

Chapter Eight

The First Holiday

No matter how you slice it, your first holiday without your husband will probably be hard. And oddly, there's no real way to prepare yourself for this, other than to expect a feeling of sadness and not blame yourself for it.

My first holiday without Jack was Valentine's Day, February 14. I'd been a widow about six weeks, and thought I could handle it—Valentine's Day is just one day, after all. My friend Marie, also a widow, invited me to have dinner with her and some other women, but I didn't know them all so I said no. That may have been a mistake. Instead I booked a hotel room in Cocoa Beach, on the ocean—I'd had success with my trip to Key Largo, after all, and this was a whole month later.

Valentine's Day fell on a Monday, so I decided to stay Saturday and Sunday night, checking out at noon on Valentine's Day and driving home slowly, taking my time. Maybe I'd stop along the way for lunch, I thought, or—maybe not.

My weekend went beautifully on Saturday and Sunday. I lounged by the pool, swam laps and ordered room service both nights. There's nothing like room service if you want a little extra pampering.

Monday morning I was fine, dry-eyed and energetic, checking out and loading my bag into the car. The desk clerk was giving everyone a flower upon check out, and that was alright too, although it did remind me, once again, what day it was. I started driving home slowly listening to oldie goldies on the radio, until I noticed they were mostly love songs—then I turned the radio off. It's Valentine's Day, I told myself matter-of-factly—what can you expect?

I was hungry as I approached New Smyrna Beach and thought I'd stop for lunch. Monday afternoon, about 2 p.m.—just like any other day, right?

Wrong. As I pulled into the parking lot of Norwood's restaurant I realized how packed the place was. It's a very good restaurant, I thought— of course they're going to do a great business on...Valentine's Day. Bucking up, I went inside.

Inside, I was seated at a table for two in the main dining area. The room was festive and pretty; every table was occupied with loving couples of all ages, out to celebrate Valentine's Day. Some of the women had flowers, and others were quite dressed up. Ordinarily, such a scene would delight my senses, but suddenly, looking around, I felt my eyes fill with tears.

It was Valentine's Day, and I was alone. My husband was gone, and I was alone.

Wiping my eyes, I ordered a glass of wine and the lunch special, crab cakes. By the time my lunch arrived, tears were running down my cheeks; I had to avert my face from the waitress's sympathetic glance. I gulped my meal in between gasps and sobs, and left, leaving an enormous tip.

Inside my car I really broke down. Crying my eyes out all the way home, I was aware of the hurt in my chest, and the strange feeling of disorientation I'd experienced so often in the last six weeks.

But mostly I was aware of missing Jack. Oh please, please! I sobbed, as if begging him to come back. But I knew he wouldn't be back. My dear husband was gone.

Yet this story, believe it or not, has a happy ending. Arriving home at 5 p.m. I found a rather large package on my doorstep. At first I thought it was a sweater I'd ordered from Coldwater Creek. (Remember my advice to order stuff from catalogues?)

That would have been nice enough, but carrying the box into my bedroom, I noticed it was postmarked New York.

I opened it up. Inside was a gorgeous silk scarf from the Metropolitan Museum of Art, along with a set of five floral postcards, a decorative pen, some scented soap and body wash—all from an old friend, Victoria, whom I'd known 25 years. We'd spoken for an hour on the phone the week before, and, kind woman that she is, she'd sent me a beautiful gift for Valentine's Day.

I've received many gifts in my life, but few have been as welcome (and as perfectly timed) as Victoria's extravagant potpourri of presents from the MET. And in the end, isn't a caring friend the best Valentine's gift of all?

Guildelines for Handling the First Holiday

1. Don't overestimate your ability to handle your first holiday alone—no matter how well you've been coping, it may be tougher than you expect.

2. If possible, try to spend the first holiday with loving friends or relatives who are aware of what you're going through, and who will pamper you the whole day.

3. Plan a special treat for yourself—if nothing else, order something online or from a catalogue that will arrive at about the time of the holiday.

4. Don't try to be superwoman like I did, and dine alone on a holiday—at least not the first one. This is not the time to experience your independence.

5. Acknowledge to yourself before the day or season begins that it *is* a holiday—it's not just another day. (Don't let it bite you in the butt, like it did me!)

Chapter Nine

Prayer

I couldn't have gotten through the early stages of widowhood without prayer. I've relied on prayer in tough situations for many years, and widowhood is a tough situation. My friend Anne prayed for me when my husband was in the hospital (and for him too, of course), and she continued after he died. Just knowing someone else was thinking about me in this supportive way was comforting.

If you are not a believer in prayer, you're welcome to skip this chapter (or jump down to the "List of Blessings"). If you do turn to prayer, or would like to, let me say that ongoing prayer, a sort of dialogue with a higher power, can do wonders for getting you through the day.

For many years I've used the Jabez prayer for strength and comfort. Jabez, evidently a rather unimportant figure in the Old Testament (he's only mentioned twice), nevertheless supplied a powerful prayer that really touches all the important bases:

> O God, if you will bless me indeed
>
> And enlarge my coast
>
> And that your hand will guide me
>
> And keep me from evil
>
> That it may not grieve me, Amen.

> (1 Chronicles 4:10)

The Jabez prayer has become a world phenomenon, because of its remarkable effectiveness. You can pray it for yourself, or you can add the names of friends, relatives or world situations as the object of your prayer, and of course, you can add your husband's name.

The Lord's Prayer is preferred by Christians, and it too asks the powers that be for protection from evil:

Our Father, which art in heaven,

Hallowed be thy name.

Thy kingdom come, thy will be done,

On earth as it is in heaven.

Give us this day, our daily bread,

And forgive us our debts,

As we forgive our debtors.

And lead us not into temptation,

But deliver us from evil.

(Matthew 6:9)

I often use my own prayers, and they are typically based on my List of Blessings. If you feel uncomfortable with a formal prayer, but would like some meditative comfort during the day, I suggest you try this.

Find yourself a soothing spot to sit where you can write in a notebook or journal (yes, a computer will do just fine). Start with a state of gratitude, as mentioned in Chapter 2, and then write down every single thing you are grateful for. Take a look at my "List of Blessings" in the Appendix to give you an idea.

There are other forms of prayer you can avail yourself of no matter what your religious orientation of lack thereof. You can take a walk through the park and commune with the trees, enjoying the silence of nature and its mystical, enchanting benevolence. You can go to the beach (a hot day is best) and immerse yourself in the ocean, feeling enveloped in a force bigger than you, yet soft to the touch. Or, if the water's too cold to go in, walk along the shore at dusk or sunrise—there's a strange sensation of being on the top of the world, and almost weightless that occurs as you drift. You can practically see the curvature of the earth, or so it seems. If you live near the mountains, take a drive on a winding mountain road in the early morning, when the sun sparkling through the trees can't help but lift your saddened heart. City dwellers can visit a museum or gallery—fine art is known for its healing qualities, and admiring the beauty of a Monet or Renoir can be a form of prayer.

Have you done any of these things in former days? Then yes, in my estimation you have prayed—you have felt your oneness with nature and mankind. In your fragile state, now is the time to make use of prayer again to heal you—any way you can.

Guidelines for Letting Prayer Heal You

1. Take a walk on the beach, in a park, or on a country road, and as you do, try saying the Jabez prayer. Each day add more people to the list of those you bless. (For further details, consult *The Prayer of Jabez*, by Dr. Bruce Wilkinson.)

2. Make a "List of Blessings," writing down as many as you can, as quickly as you can. This is particularly good for "down" days, when you just don't think you can go on.

3. Write your own prayer. This is particularly good if you're unsure of your feelings about religion or spirituality, but you're feeling lots of emotion anyway. Your prayer might be something like this:

   I will strive, every day, to put sorrow behind me. I willremember the wonderful things about my husband,

and try to honor his memory. I will think kindly and positivelyabout myself, and try to help people when I can.

Some people would call this prayer an *affirmation*—but if that strikes you as too New Age, you don't have to call it anything. Personally, I like the idea of an affirmation—we are affirming something positive about ourselves. There's nothing wrong with that.

4. Before going to bed at night, listen to some peaceful music, and think grateful thoughts.

5. Find a Church, Synagogue, Temple, Mosque, or Ashram. Visit, even if you're not a member.

6. Get out in the yard and do some gardening, focusing only on what you're doing, so that each planting of a flower or bush becomes an act of worship.

7. Do the same in the kitchen, chopping vegetables, or baking a pie.

8. Volunteer to read at a children's hospital or nursing home, or do something to help the homeless.

9. Go to a museum or art gallery, and find a favorite painting—an Impressionist work is wonderful for this—and let yourself flow into the artwork. Try to capture the essence of beauty in the painting, even the artist's intention if you're able, and appreciate it.

10. Take a favorite aunt, uncle, sister-in-law or friend, someone who doesn't get out too much, to lunch or dinner at a special place. Make a fuss over this individual, letting the person know how much you like him or her. (Yes, this sounds a bit like "do something nice for someone"—but can we ever really have too much *nice*?)

Chapter Ten

Let People Help You

Most of us these days are used to being independent, free-thinking individuals, and are quite used to taking care of ourselves. We've had careers, sometimes with a high level of responsibility; we've managed homes, raised children, and most recently, acted as caretakers for our husbands if there was a need to do this. Accustomed to the labels of "super-woman" and "having it all," we may find it a bit of a shock to discover ourselves feeling needy and worse, sometimes unable to do the things we used to take care of easily.

Grief, unfortunately, can be incapacitating. I've mentioned the strange state of disorientation that can occur, where you can't think, and literally don't know what to do next. Equally as perplexing is a state I call "Helpless Hannah" (or it could be called Helpless Joanna)—a condition that I found overtaking me at times when I just couldn't make things work. The simplest tasks were suddenly overwhelming: vacuuming the living room, taking out the garbage, dealing with a seemingly endless number of computer snafus.

If you're experiencing any of this, relax—it's only temporary. Don't allow yourself to suffer because of unresolved situations that can be easily handled by someone else: Let people help you.

We like to think we can handle everything alone, even grief. Sure, we'll allow friends and relatives to take us out to dinner, and listen to us reminisce about our loved one, but when it comes to dealing with day to day tasks, we'll do them ourselves, thank you. I have one question regarding this attitude (which I myself have always displayed, so I know how ingrained it can be)—why? Why suffer trying to take care of some little job that you can't handle because grief got in your eyes, when someone else can take care of the situation in minutes?

Let me give you some examples. Right at the point when I was finishing up the editing of my friend Karen's book—about 6 ½ months after Jack passed away—my computer suddenly appeared to "crash." The screen went blank, strange and ominous messages appeared telling me to consult a website immediately (which I couldn't do because the computer was now dormant, useless, a frozen lump of dark screen). Trying not to panic, I tried "fixing" the computer—pressing every button I could think of, such as unplugging the computer, but nothing seemed to make any difference.

Now, previously in such situations, I'd ask my husband to take a look, and he'd eventually fix the problem. It's okay to ask your husband to fix things, because that's what they do, right? Husbands fix things. But I no longer had a husband, and at the moment, I couldn't think of any friend who could fix a crashed computer. In fact—I couldn't think, period.

That's the give-away sign, ladies—when you can't think. Finally, I gave up and went out to lunch. Over stuffed mushrooms and Caesar salad, I prayed, and then wrote in my journal. Returning home, I checked the computer—still black, but stuck in the on position—then, I prepared to call a computer repair place and shell out a couple hundred bucks. Then suddenly, I thought of my husband's cousin's son, Pete. I hadn't seen him in at least five months, had no idea what he was up to or if he was in town, but I knew he was computer savvy (and he'd once told me to call if I ever needed computer help).

I found his number and called him—he answered on the second ring. He offered to come over in an hour and take a look, but first suggested I hold the off/on button down for 20 seconds.

You guessed it; that simple little step turned the computer off, and I was able to restart it immediately. I was back in business.

I'm mentioning this, because, superwoman that we all are, we may not think of turning to others to solve simple problems or take care of basic needs. We've always done it before (with the help of hubby, at times, but nobody has to know about that). Others want to help—and as I've mentioned earlier, people are very nice to widows. They want to make things right for us, but they're not mind-readers—we need to ask for assistance.

In another computer-related incident, I was rushing to prepare to go back to work after 7 ½ months of widowhood. I'd just joined Facebook (more on that later), and in between preparing syllabi, I was trying to log some of the basic personal information onto my profile page.

Suddenly, to my horror, I found I had a huge typo, and I couldn't seem to correct it. Other information was askew as well—I finally gave up, almost laughing at the foolishness of the situation (except that I'm teaching writing, and a typo, for me, is well, *unforgiveable*).

What did I do? I went shopping. (Shopping, as you recall, is one of my main remedies, in times of trouble.) While out and about, I thought of my friend Cheryl, who'd offered to help me set up a link on my Facebook page to a special page for a students' blog, or anything else I'd like. I was a little reluctant to call Cheryl for such a silly request, but we'd always been close, and she had offered to help...

When I got home, I called her—she answered the phone immediately, always a good sign, and of course, agreed to help me. After an hour long chat, we hung up—my Facebook page was fixed 20 minutes later.

I'm giving these examples to show not just how we can be thrown by very simple problems while in the grieving state, but also to illustrate how easily they can be fixed by putting pride and stoicism aside—and letting someone else help you.

So don't suffer alone, do without, or pay strangers to do things your friends and family might easily take care of for you—if you just ask.

Guidelines for Letting People Help You

1. Recognize that an inability to do simple tasks does not mean you're losing your mind or succumbing to early Alzheimer's. Grief strikes every fiber of your being—including your thought processes.

2. When you find yourself unable to handle something, reach out to someone you know for help. Pick up the phone, email a friend, or walk next door to a neighbor's house, and explain what you need.

3. Flickering thoughts of "I should be able to handle this," or "she'll think I'm stupid if I ask for help" should be put aside. People want to help, and your reluctance is just your ego, balking at not being forever superwoman.

4. Yes, you can try to fix the drain, the light switch, or the ceiling fan yourself—but if it appears unfixable, don't wear yourself out trying. Go out to lunch, go shopping, or go sit in the park—ideas on what to do will come to you.

5. Don't panic. Remember, we're all in this life together. You've helped people before—now it's your turn to receive help.

Chapter Eleven

Journal Writing

One of the most useful tools for dealing with grief is journal writing. If you already use a journal, you're probably well on your way to a healing. If you haven't ever tried journaling, go out right now, and buy yourself one of those pretty little books. You can get one at any gift shop, bookstore or stationary emporium for as little as $5. Or, turn on your computer, and start a new file labeled "me."

I had kept a journal for years, so I already knew it would help. The first few weeks after my husband's passing, my journal writing was pretty ragged. I'd write down inner thoughts, interrupt myself to do a grocery list on the same page, and then later, tear the grocery list out when it was time to go to the store. That's no way to treat a journal.

After a month or so, I settled down to make my journal the cozy support tool I knew it could be. My friend Helen had given me a new journal at Jack's memorial service, a lovely brown velvet covered book, perfect for winter thoughts. After writing my name, and "Journal of..." on the front sheet, I proceeded with the introductory page:

(February 15, 2011)

"Here I am, sitting in Barnes and Noble once again. A new chapter is started: I am putting sadness away. I don't know what's ahead—I'm willing to let God lead me. There is no way I can proceed without trust. I have to trust in something, and that something is God.

Usually, sitting here, I'm feeling like a writer. Today, I'm feeling like a survivor. Some people have been extraordinarily kind, like Carole, for instance, and Victoria. And Helen has turned into a much dearer friend than I could ever have hoped for. And—an invitation to come to LA to visit Wendy. I have much to be grateful for, dear God, and I am most grateful. Please continue to guide me in the way you choose. I am willing to be obedient to the path you have selected for me."

I always write a short summary introduction to a journal, so I'll know I'm beginning a new one. It's a chance to look at myself at a moment in time. "Hey! Here I am, and I'm still breathing." Many times the introductory page will be written in the Starbuck's café at Barnes and Noble, where I've purchased the journal. (This time I brought the journal with me and bought a couple of new books.) Sometimes I'll head out to a park and sit under a tree while I contemplate the world. The introduction is brief—but in my estimation, important.

Then come the daily thoughts—several pages of personal observations, commentary and reminiscences. This is the healing part: here's where you let it all out on the page, those thoughts you haven't told anyone yet. You can record here how lonely you are for your man, and how lost you feel without him. You can list all the ways you're going to spend money on yourself to heal. You can confess which neighbor is driving you nuts, or muse about whether or not that certain family friend is coming on to you. No one is going to see this—not ever. You can be honest with yourself.

Your honesty is what is going to carry you on to the next level. After a while, you may notice yourself making some plans in your journal. I suggest creating a separate page for different types of plans. My journal for February included:

1. To Do February

2. Three-month Plan for Spring (Mar-Apr-May)

3. Writing Schedule for Spring

You can substitute whatever project you're working on for #3: redecorating your bedroom, planting a garden, or finding a job. I also like to keep lists of a comforting nature in my journal. These would include:

1. New List of Nice Things to Do (mentioned earlier)

2. Good that Has Unfolded Since…(list a recent favorable occurrence)

3. List of Blessings

Samples of all these lists can be found in the Appendix.

Take the time to really invest yourself in your journal, and it will become a friend to support you throughout your widowhood. It's a friend that will never let you down.

Guidelines for Journal Writing

1. Try to write in your journal every day. The value of journal writing is cumulative. You will get more expressive, and more honest with yourself as you continue.

2. When you get an idea for something as your write in your journal—a new project, a recipe, or a gift for someone—stop, and start a list on a separate page. That way your journal will become a resource for you.

3. Use your journal to organize your emotional life. You can make lists of people you love, lists of good things that have happened in your past, and lists of things that make you happy. You can decorate these lists with illustrations and designs. (Note: you can do all this if you're keeping a journal on your computer as well.)

4. If you start repeating yourself, pay attention. If you keep writing, "I need to quit my job," or "I need to see a therapist"—that means you really want to do it.

5. Be kind to yourself in your journal. If you notice you're writing nasty things about yourself in your journal, stop. Start making a note of all you've accomplished instead.

Chapter Twelve

The Value of Grief

I've been talking a lot about how to overcome grief. The truth is, the process of grieving is extremely important, and its value should not be diminished.

It's hard to value something that is causing pain, yet pain itself is the very thing that lets us know we are alive right now. We have not died—even though, at times, we may wish we had. We may wonder if there is any value left in our life, much less in grieving. What's it all about, anyway?

I'm not a psychiatrist, but having faced three traumatic deaths, I know it is better to take your time mourning your loved one, rather than pretending it doesn't matter. I learned this the hard way when my father died.

I was 39 years old, well into my second marriage, when my mother called to tell me Dad was going into the hospital.

"It's an aneurism," she said. "The doctor said it could burst any time, so your father has to have an operation."

Worriedly, I packed my bag, telling Ray, my second husband, that I wasn't sure how long I'd be down in Florida, but that I'd call him every night. Ray apologized for not being able to leave his job, but I told him it wasn't necessary. "I'm sure he'll be fine," I said, mostly to convince myself.

But my father wasn't fine. He survived the operation, only to be told that he'd have to have one of his legs amputated—diabetes had set in. Mother and I were horrified, but Dad agreed to the operation. He wanted to live.

After the amputation, his spirits seemed to flag—he'd been such an active man. I had been down in Florida now almost a month, and thought I'd better go check on Ray and the state of our household.

"I'll be back in two days," I told my father, holding his hand by the hospital bed.

"Jodie, don't leave," he said hoarsely. "If you leave, I'll die."

I was taken aback—the doctors had all agreed that Dad was recovering nicely. "I'll be right back," I said. "I'll be back on Sunday. I love you."

He shut his eyes and turned his head away. Bewildered, I kissed his somewhat damp forehead and left the room, heading out to a waiting taxi. Four hours later I was in New York, soothing my husband who was dealing with a major business situation, and paying the household bills.

On Sunday, I was back at LaGuardia, waiting to board my plane. A bit early, I decided to give Mom a call. It took a long time for the nurses to find her. When she finally got on the phone, her voice was strained. "Your father died two hours ago," she told me. "He contracted pneumonia last night—there was nothing anyone could do."

That was the start of the biggest nightmare of my life. Guilt poured through me like scalding coffee, turning me into a mass of nerves. There were many unresolved issues with my father—his final words to me were just the tip of the iceberg. After the funeral, things got worse: first, a rash broke out all over my body that took weeks to heal. Then, much more traumatic, I plunged into a depression that had me throwing away all the knives and scissors in the house, for fear of hurting myself.

In between those two events—the rash and the depression, I had about five months in which I could have grieved for my father, seeking the help of a therapist, since I obviously needed one. But I didn't. I tried to pretend there was nothing wrong—going to parties, and resuming my old life with very little thought for my father. When the depression finally hit, it was like being ambushed—I couldn't eat, couldn't sleep, and couldn't even think most of the time. When I finally called a therapist, it was that, or check into the Kings Park Psychiatric Center—and if I'd done that, I might not have come out.

A year and a half of therapy later, I was better but still shaky. I'd begun writing again, after a hiatus of about eight months. I had learned—the hard way—how to do some self-nurturing, and the guilt of unresolved issues with my father had begun to subside.

Then, two years after my father's death, another trauma. In the middle of the night, I received a call from a doctor, telling me that my mother was in a coma. She'd gone to a clinic for cosmetic surgery—first a face-lift, then a tummy tuck. The face-lift had gone well; the tummy tuck hadn't. In shock, Ray and I rushed to Florida, my brother Robert traveling from Seattle to meet us at the hospital. Mom was in a coma a week before she died—my brother and I had to make the decision to remove her life support.

This time, I knew better then to carry on with business as usual. I allowed myself a full grieving process, with everything that entails. I was still in therapy, thankfully, and I had some very supportive friends. I did not go into a depression, because I knew what to do: allow grief to move in with me for a while.

And so, some 20 plus years later, I was somewhat prepared to deal with the death of my dear husband, Jack. Jack was my soul mate. We met in 1968, got married in '69, and had a wild ride through the next decade as political hippies. Maybe we got a little too wild, because we didn't make it to the 80s; we divorced that year, and I married Ray. But Jack and I remained friends, and in 1989, we got back together, tying the knot again in 1994. Jack was my first love—and my last. I miss him terribly, but I've learned how to grieve, to let the pain have its way with you till it wears itself out. It will ebb slowly, if you give it its due, but, as my friend Charlotte, herself a widow, is quick to point out, it never goes away completely.

The night before Jack died, we had returned from the hospital late, after what was reportedly a false alarm. A home health care nurse said she wasn't getting an adequate pulse from Jack's wrist; we rushed to the emergency room, but once there, it seemed all Jack's vitals were stable. Relieved, and rejoicing, we returned home—it was New Year's Day, the first day of 2011. We ate a belated New Year's dinner—turkey, mashed potatoes, and green beans—Jack, of course, could eat very little. He'd been in and out of the hospital most of the latter part of December, a very sick man.

After dinner, we both dozed on the couch for a while, exhausted. Waking around midnight, I suggested going to bed. Jack agreed, but collapsed back on the couch when he tried to stand.

"Lean on me," I suggested, helping him up. The two of us made our way to the bedroom—I was almost carrying Jack, he weighed so little now, but of course, it was still a tremendous effort.

When we reached the bedroom, and Jack was settled in bed, he reached for my hand: "I want you to know how much I appreciate what you just did," he said, gasping. "That must have been hard."

"Oh no," I demurred, sitting down beside him. "It wasn't that bad—I love you."

"I love you too," he whispered, shutting his eyes.

He died the next day. Our last intimate scene, and our words to each other will stay in my mind forever, often bringing tears to my eyes.

Jack was always such a grateful man.

Guidelines for Understanding the Value of Grief

1. When a loved one dies, particularly a husband, don't try to carry on with "business as usual." Even if you have a job, make some adjustments. Take time off, go away on the weekends, and realize that you are in a vulnerable state.

2. Make a plan as soon as possible, working in plenty of time to contemplate and mourn your loss.

3. Read books concerned with grieving; see movies where someone dies (movies can provide a genuinely cathartic experience for you). And once again, crying is absolutely necessary; cry as much as you want to.

4. Take your time with your grieving—there is no rush. Let God heal you.

5. Write about your grieving process. There are few better ways to heal than writing about your feelings.

Part Two:
Learning to Take Care of Yourself

Chapter Thirteen

Rituals

This morning, I woke up, made coffee and treated myself to a delicious cream puff I'd purchased the day before from the Publix bakery. It was Sunday, and I always made sure I had some special delicacy to enjoy with my morning coffee on this day that no-work-can-be-done.

Enjoying some savory treat on Sunday morning was a ritual I'd carried out with my husband for many years. Some Sundays, we devoured apple turnovers; others, it was a flakey croissant with raspberry jam. I'd make sure our treat was different every week, and Jack would greet each dish with ooh's and ah's of delight.

The tendency is, of course, to abandon such rituals, now that you're a widow with no husband to share them with. Don't do it. It's hard enough to be without your husband; why should you punish yourself by taking away the little treats and ceremonies you've obviously gotten used to? Is there really any virtue in settling for a cup of tea and a hard-boiled egg on Sunday mornings, when you used to eat cream puffs?

"But, it'll make me miss him even more!" you wail, walking resolutely past the bakery counter where the familiar cream puffs, Napoleons, and blueberry-cheese strudels reside.

Possibly. It probably will make you think of your husband, and how much fun it was to enjoy those croissants together. How your dear one always commented on how large the croissants were—"It's the biggest I've ever seen!" he'd say, every time you served him one. Yes, you'll probably think of that, but you'll remember it fondly, as you lick the strawberry jam off your fingers.

Don't punish yourself because your husband is no longer around. I know widows who have stopped cooking altogether. Not a good idea, I'd say. This is the time to treat yourself well, not deprive yourself of the good things you've gotten used to.

Did you and your husband go out to a favorite place on Sunday afternoons and listen to music or watch a ball game? Did you go dancing Saturday nights, or to a movie? Was Thursday your bowling night? Try to find a way to continue some of these activities—with a girlfriend or two, or by yourself if necessary. Not everything you did with your husband will be possible to repeat, of course—and I'm not just talking about activities in the bedroom. But make an effort, please. After all, you're still here—and you still *like* going to the movies, don't you?

Having a drink to end the week on Friday night, going to the Farmer's Market on Saturday mornings, or having French toast on the weekend—these are little things you can and should continue. Yes, you may feel uncomfortable at first—but after a while, it will seem natural, and it may even become something you're doing to honor the memory of your loved one. That's what a ritual is all about, really.

Guidelines for Rituals

1. Cook something your husband especially liked, and serve it to yourself as a special meal. Or, if he liked to cook, make one of his specialties.

2. Visit a place where the two of you used to hang out— the beach, a special restaurant, the tennis court, or a fishing pier. Propose a toast to your husband to

acknowledge your love for him. (It's okay to do this with a friend, as long as it's someone who understands grieving.)

3. Wear an outfit your husband liked, and go someplace special the two of you frequented.

4. Choose one activity you and your husband enjoyed together and continue it; it could be golf, square dancing, or even visiting the public library.

5. Find a photograph of your husband and figure out a way to greet it in the morning. My husband's funeral home gave me a laminated bookmark with his photo, which I use in my journal. Every morning, I touch that photo—no matter how quick the touch (or sometimes the kiss), I feel I've made a connection with the love I had for my husband.

Chapter Fourteen

Making Household Repairs

Finding yourself a new widow is like starting a journey: you know where you are now (you're without your husband), but you don't exactly know what you'll feel like when you reach your destination. Will you be peaceful? Relieved? Not too sure if you really want to be there?

Of course, widowhood differs from a journey in that you can't just throw up your hands and say, "I don't really like this. I think I'll go back to where I came from."

No, you can't do that, dear—you can't go back to having your hubby around, no matter how much you wish you could. Sometimes, the condition of being a widow seems so unreal that it almost feels like you could make that choice: "No, I don't care for this experience. I'd like to go back to my real life, please."

Like it or not, widowhood is your real life now. This feeling of unreality, as if you'll turn a corner and be back to your old self again—your self with him—may last weeks, or even months. You may think you've conquered it, only to have that strange, slightly eerie sensation pop up when you least expect it—at the grocery store, for instance, or in the middle of a household repair.

I'd been a widow for about four months, and from my friends' comments, felt I was coping pretty well. One day, I had a load of laundry in the dryer: sheets, towels, and the whole she-bang. I opened the door to the laundry room to get something out of the adjoining bathroom, and was hit with the strong smell of burning oil. Ugh. Instantly I thought of Jack's caution that the dryer ventilator must be kept hydrated: that is—water had to be poured into a little container periodically so that the vent didn't get too hot.

Gingerly I got out a ladder and set it up. I didn't much like ladders, especially when I had to climb them while holding something in my hand. But it had to be done, so I filled a small saucepan with water, made my way up the ladder and tipped the saucepan until the water poured into the vent container. I climbed back down, put the ladder away and started the dryer again, feeling quite proud of myself. "Let's see if that helps," I muttered.

I came back five minutes later to check. The oil smell was still there. "Hmm, what's going on?" I wondered. "We don't use oil heat..."

We. Did you catch it? It's not uncommon to think of yourself as "we" even after four months, especially when it comes to something your husband was actively involved in. Jack always refilled the water. Fortunately, I was smart enough to watch how he did it—but not until the last year of his life.

I chuckled to myself, noting my use of the word "we" in this situation, and my laugh alleviated whatever nervousness I was experiencing about the whole thing. I started the dryer again to see if the odor was still there. It was—but fading.

Ten minutes later the smell of oil had completely gone. I had completed a repair, the first of many I was to master in my first year of widowhood. Maybe having the "we" along for those first few household fixes isn't such a bad idea.

Guidelines for Mastering Household Repairs

1. Tackle each repair as it comes up, trusting in "serendipity." If something needs fixing at a particular moment, it's because you now have the ability to fix it.

2. If you feel nervous, it's okay to ask yourself what your husband would do. After all, you have to learn somehow.

3. Think the repair out completely in your mind, from beginning to end. Don't plunge in blindly. (You don't do other things "blindly," so why handle a repair that way?)

4. It's okay to call someone if the repair is beyond you. There's no need to turn into a macho superwoman about household repairs (even if you're that way about everything else in your life).

5. Congratulate yourself after you've completed a household repair. It will probably be the first of many—and you've handled it alone, without a man. Give yourself a treat!

Chapter Fifteen

Lunching Out

I'm at the Topaz Hotel in Flagler Beach, having lunch. Since I'm a widow, and still wearing a wedding ring, I do not feel funny being alone. No, I don't announce myself to all I meet as a "widow, recently bereaved"—but I know it. I used to go out for lunch or coffee often when Jack was alive, but I always felt a little guilty, even if he was working (and more so the last years of his life, when he was nearly bedridden). Even though he urged me to go out and enjoy myself, I'd still feel guilty.

Now, I have no reason to feel any guilt. I trust Jack is happy wherever he is—I have to believe that for my own peace of mind, and I do. As for me—I may not feel exactly happy, but I am content with myself and my status. In this lovely restaurant, outside on the veranda, looking at the ocean across the street, I at least know who I am.

It's very different from being single after a divorce. As I recall, I didn't much like going out by myself at that time, and I usually rounded up a girlfriend or two. Now, however, I can sit here, looking out at pink bougainvillea and slightly swaying palm trees and not feel the least bit uncomfortable that I am alone. Yes, I've spent plenty of time with women friends in the last few months, but the very word "widow" means that I am alone, without a spouse, and it's okay.

The trick to going out alone, comfortably and without trepidation, is, first of all, to look good. Dress as carefully as you would if you were with a friend—makeup, hair done, a nice shirt and pants, perhaps a jacket or tunic. If you are like me, at just four months you don't have much interest in attracting male attention—yet you want to be presentable when you look in a mirror. You want to be reassured that the reflection you get back is acceptable to you. More than that, you are *going out*, not running to the grocery store to buy some detergent (some of us, of course, put on lipstick to go to the grocery store, but that's another issue.) Today I'm wearing a black linen short-sleeved shirt, and tan slacks, with silver jewelry and my new summer handbag made of straw and black leather. I love the handbag, even though it was a bit of a splurge.

Anyway, you are out in the world, just as you were with your husband—only he's not there at the moment. That's one way to look at it, and I'm not advocating having conversations with dead spouses. I'm merely saying, you're out having lunch, or a coffee, or a drink—make yourself look nice, even if you're alone, most especially if you're alone. Learning to go out alone is key to developing a satisfactory widowhood, as important as learning to cook meals for yourself.

My lunch today at the Topaz is more than satisfactory; it is delicious. I've just finished a salad of blackened sea scallops, goat cheese, walnuts, mandarin orange slices and a variety of lettuces, topped with a mysterious, yet delicious house dressing. It's billed as "Flagler Beach's most famous salad," and I'm sure it is. With it, a hard roll and butter in the shape of a scallop. This lunch has been a very good experience—not that the entrée was so unusual, but it was prepared perfectly. I'm also glad I wore my short-sleeved top, because out here on the veranda it's warm—deliciously warm.

If this is being a widow, it is a blessed and holy state. Waves are lapping onto the shore in the blue sea across A1A. Fragrances of all sorts—from flowers to scented soap—waft past my nostrils. Now, the taste of coffee, sweetened just right, and soon—crème brulee.

The crème brulee arrives and is sublime. Perhaps I didn't need it; perhaps the coffee would have been enough. Yet I indulged, just for the sake of indulging.

Eventually, I will learn exactly how much to accept in every situation. Eventually, I will learn balance again, but right now, I am lunching out, and I am having dessert. I look good, and I'm having dessert. I'm saying a lot, aren't I? If you're a new widow, you know what I mean.

Guildelines for Lunching Out

1. Choose restaurants that you can afford. You want to be able to order anything on the menu comfortably, without having to worry about your budget. (You can worry about your budget later—this is the time for treating yourself abundantly.)

2. Dress yourself well. Wear jewelry, makeup, and a pretty, yet comfortable, outfit. (No tight waistbands, please!) Dress as if you were going out to lunch with someone special. You are.

3. Allow plenty of time. It's better, especially for your first lunching out experience, to go out on a Saturday, rather than try and squeeze in this special experience on your lunch hour at work. Give yourself at least an hour and a half to daydream and enjoy yourself.

4. It's okay to carry a notepad or something to write on (your iphone will do), but try to resist the temptation to take a book. You want to experience the feeling of you eating lunch in your chosen environment, not escape to a fictional world.

5. Order dessert your first time lunching out, even if you're on a diet. There's something about adding a

luscious dessert to the end of your meal that says, "Yes, I love you, and I'm giving you a special treat!"

Chapter Sixteen

Lists

How do you get by, day to day, accomplishing what you have to accomplish, when your heart is broken? It's not easy, but there is one tool (a lifesaving tool, I'd say), that will invariably work, no matter how upset you are on any particular day.

That tool is *lists*. Almost everyone uses some kind of list: grocery lists, things-to-do lists, lists of people to invite to events. The type of lists I'm referring to for this particular time in your life goes beyond this. I'm talking about life-managing lists, where you write down what you want to do during every hour of every day. Some of us, with hectic jobs, have operated in this mode before. For a new widow who often doesn't know what she's thinking, much less what she's doing, an hourly list can be a life-saver.

Sound regimented? Yes, it is—but that's the point. You are *managing* yourself here, knowing that during the day your emotions may take a nose dive, rendering you incapable of deciding what to have for lunch, much less which bills to pay, what home repairs to tackle, or which jobs to apply for. So, knowing that you may lapse into a semi-stymied state, you take care of yourself—you manage your day with a list.

Start with a monthly list, where you write down everything you'd like to accomplish in the month ahead as detailed as you can, listing phone numbers and email addresses as needed. (I usually make this list on a Sunday afternoon, after I've been well pampered by a strawberry cheese strudel and coffee, or maybe a Swiss cheese omelet.) In other words, choose a relaxed moment to make this list, because it will guide you in the rest of your list making.

From your monthly list, create a weekly list. I made all my lists in my journal, but you can do list making on the computer, on your iphone or with any other method that works for you. Your weekly list won't have as much detail in the way of phone numbers or email addresses, but it will have specific things you want to accomplish each day of the week. Be sure to include some fun things here too—like going to a movie on Tuesday afternoon (did you know many movie theaters offer $5 Tuesdays now?) or even jotting down a special TV show you'd like to watch. Try to get the whole week mapped out on one page so you can review it at a glance. Leave a few blank spaces too, so you can fill in things as they come up. The idea is not to limit yourself, but to provide a wealth of activities, so you won't have to sink into the proverbial black hole, unable to think of what to do next.

Now comes the most challenging part—the daily list. This has to be done in the morning each day, or, if you're very upset, and evenings provide more calm, the night before. I suggest starting at 8 a.m. or earlier, no later than 9 a.m., and listing every single thing you'd like to do that day, allowing plenty of time to do it. Don't list too much—that's not the purpose of the daily list. The purpose is to keep you grounded, and to give structure to your day, so that when that awful fog in the head hits, you won't cave in. Instead, you'll consult your list, no matter how you feel, and carry on. This is time management; it's also Zen Buddhism, practical philosophy and just plain common sense. We can't live our lives based on our feelings, especially if our feelings at a particular moment aren't supporting us. Your strength, your mind, and your spirit will support you in the form of a list, which you follow, no matter how you feel. Following the list, you immediately pull yourself out of your head (which may not be a comfortable spot right now), and focus your attention on activities outside yourself. This relieves the sensation of being out of control and incapable of taking any action at all. With a list, you need not decide what to do—you just obey your wiser self (you, in a calm, peaceful state).

Did I mention the pleasure of checking things off your list?

Guidelines for Creating Lists

1. Be realistic when making your lists. The object is not to cram as much on a list as you can, but to selectively list things you'd really like to accomplish.

2. Be sure to list some enjoyable things on each schedule. A typical weekly list of mine would schedule a trip to Seashore National Part, dinner with at least two friends, and a visit to the Christian Science Reading Room—in addition to the myriad of tasks that must be accomplished.

3. Choose a calm moment to make your lists—especially if you're experiencing stress.

4. If something doesn't get done one day, list it for the following day. (I often list things twice if I'm doubtful that I'll want to do them.)

5. Relish your lists; love your lists! They will keep you sane and happy.

Chapter Seventeen

Your Birthday

Of all the holidays that can throw you for a loop, your birthday has the most potential to do just that. First, you'll either be suffering or celebrating on your own—even if you're with a roomful of people, it's unlikely there's another widow with your exact birthday at the party, so no one can know exactly how you feel. Second, if you decide to celebrate, you're going to feel that something's missing. It is—your husband.

Since my birthday came less than three months after Jack died, I knew I had to take strong measures in order not to succumb to the birthday blues. My friend Marie wanted to throw "just a little party," but I didn't think I was ready for that. I felt a gathering of people would only emphasize who wasn't there—Jack. So, following my plan of what had worked the first two months, I made a reservation at a spa on the ocean—the night before my birthday was the full moon, and I thought it would be beautiful, gazing at the moon over the dark blue ocean.

I have mentioned watching the movie "Dragonfly," starring Kevin Costner, during the weekend spent at my friend Carole's house. I probably didn't mention discussing that movie with another pal, Karen, the one who was writing her spiritual autobiography. Karen took me out for a birthday lunch two days before I was due to check into the spa and bestowed two presents upon me. "Don't open these till you get to the spa," she cautioned me. "You'll see why."

Even Karen, with her psychic gifts, could not have predicted what unfolded during that magical birthday weekend. I checked into the hotel on Saturday, bringing my various birthday gifts with me. I'd booked an ocean view room, but at the last minute I was given an ocean front room for two nights for just $20 more—and my room was breathtaking. That night at dusk, I opened the French doors onto the balcony and lay down on my canopied bed. As the sky slowly turned from blue to pink to orange, I fell into a state of semi-sleep. I heard a noise, and opened my eyes to see something flying over my bed. I sat up in amazement: it was a dragonfly! Even in the dusk, the luminous wings were unmistakable.

"Gosh!" I whispered, climbing out of bed to follow the dragonfly as it circled the room, and then flew back out through the French doors and away, toward the sea.

The moon was coming up over the ocean now—a huge, red full moon, like none I'd ever seen. Shivers went down my spin as I stood on the balcony bathed in the soft red moonglow. It was a night of enchantment, and I couldn't help but wonder, just as in the movie: *Was that Jack who'd come to visit me in the form of a dragonfly?*

There were more surprises the following day. I opened my presents on the balcony after breakfasting on French toast with strawberries, bacon, orange juice and coffee. There was a box full of goodies from Marie: two scarves, a necklace and a blouse from my favorite store, Coldwater Creek. My brother Robert had sent an edible potpourri of treats: cookies, cheeses, assorted crackers, and candy. From Carole, I got a wonderful, inspiring book titled, *Praying from the Heart,* edited by James Stuart Bell. My sister in law Mary Jo had outdone herself with a beautiful angel candle and scented oils; Victoria had sent note cards and a gorgeous scarf in a design from Louis Comfort Tiffany.

But it was Karen's gifts that really threw me for a loop, and made me think that maybe I wasn't celebrating my birthday *alone* after all. Her first gift was a pretty journal, into which she'd stuffed typed messages of inspiration. Opening the second gift, I was aware of a strange sensation of déjà vu, as if I were watching myself perform this ritual from some high-up place miles above the hotel balcony. My feelings toward the "Joanna" opening the birthday presents below were fondness and compassion, with just a tiny touch of concern.

Karen's second gift was a colorful piece of costume jewelry. At first, I wasn't quite sure what it was, so I lifted it out of its box and held it up in the light. The jewelry glittered with a piercing luminosity as the sunlight touched it.

It was a pin—in the shape of a dragonfly.

Guidelines for Handling Your Birthday

1. Don't feel conspicuous about going somewhere alone—remember, your birthday is only a holiday for you. It's not like you're going out alone on New Year's Eve.

2. Try to celebrate in a way that's meaningful to you. After all, this is the start of a new life year in a new mode.

3. Don't expect to feel the same as you have on previous birthdays—you won't. If you usually feel giddy, you may well be blue; if blue is your usual mode, you could well find yourself peaceful.

4. Accumulate some presents to open on "the day" by whatever means necessary. Save gifts that people send in advance.

5. Be grateful you are still alive.

Chapter Eighteen

Loneliness

It's late Saturday night and you're settling down to watch TV in bed. You've been on the go all day, doing chores, errands, and tasks connected with your job, or maybe even doing some shopping for yourself. You've been out with the girls the previous night, and tomorrow there's a brunch for a friend from out of town—no, you're not socially deprived. But suddenly, you're hit with "it"—almost as if the wind had been knocked out of you.

You know what "it" is—loneliness. You've felt it before, often in fact, but you'd thought it was easing up. Yet there it is—that queasy, almost nauseous feeling, and the slight sense of disorientation, as if you're not quite sure who you are. Loneliness—there's nothing you can do about it.

You don't feel lonely with friends, and you think it may have been a mistake to let a Saturday night creep up on you without social plans. Saturday night, date night. When your husband was alive you went out on Saturday night—didn't you?

No, not always. In fact, in recent years, Jack and I usually went out on Friday nights and Sunday afternoons. We began to look forward to Saturday evenings in—Jack loved to cook, and he'd try out new recipes. As he became more ill, he'd still want to share some things he'd discovered on the cooking channel, such as one of those lovely Asian fusion dishes.

So, why the panic? In a way that's what it is, a low-grade panic attack—about being home alone on Saturday night.

It's precisely because you are now deprived of whatever it was you did together on Saturday, Sunday, or whatever other day is causing you pain. If you stayed home and watched a movie together, just the act of settling down on the sofa or making the popcorn can cause an upset, because it will remind you that you're watching the movie without your husband. So, staying home can bring you just as much pain as driving by someplace you used to go with your husband. You can't win.

Or can you? Once again, facing the situation squarely and frankly is probably the best remedy. Admit that you have pain. Admit that you are now alone after 10, 15, 25, or 50 years of being with your husband. It's too soon to be a social butterfly, no matter how much you may like to think of yourself that way. You are a widow, and you are alone.

There, you've said it. It's not so bad, is it? After all, when your husband was alive you weren't out socializing every single minute. Weren't there times when it was cozy just to be home, in your comfortable, familiar surroundings, even if all you were doing was reading a book?

Actually, reading a book is a good idea in times of loneliness. It might be better than TV (unless there's a really good movie on). Other things you can do to combat loneliness at home are: cooking something delicious; writing in your journal; making a plan for the coming week; browsing through catalogues and picking out clothes you'd like to buy; looking up stuff on the Internet of a frivolous nature, like astrology charts or new hair styles; cleaning out your dresser drawers or messy desk (try it!); doing some sewing; painting a picture; sending out Facebook friend invites; calling someone on the phone; meditating; giving yourself a manicure; planning a vacation; looking up courses to take at a local college; listening to music; baking some cookies; taking a bubble bath, or writing a poem.

Any of these will ease your loneliness, and might be more enjoyable than TV. (That is, unless there's a *really* good movie on.)

Guidelines for Dealing with Loneliness

1. If you're lonely, call it for what it is. You're not sick, mentally unbalanced, unpopular, helpless, or "stuck" in your situation. You're a new widow. You're lonely.

2. Realize that this situation will get better, but it may take a while. In the larger scheme of things, it doesn't speak too well of your marriage if you *don't* miss your husband a little, right?

3. If you're going through a bout of loneliness, line up some friends to spend extra time with. They'll certainly understand.

4. If you do find yourself faced with an unwanted or unexpected evening at home, prepare something to do as soon as possible. Plan an unusual dinner to make (nothing too hard, just good!), or set up a little project for yourself, like those mentioned above.

5. Use the time to get to know yourself. If you can really, truly make friends with *you*, you'll never be lonely again.

Chapter Nineteen

Facebook

It's all so familiar, isn't it—the cute little thumbs up, the ongoing stream of (usually) happy messages—but as a newly bereaved widow, I had not yet joined Facebook. I'd wanted to—but just couldn't seem to get the energy to do it. Then, when I went up to the North Carolina reunion, my friend Cheryl practically insisted Facebook was what I needed. She signed me up, and added the women at the North Carolina gathering as well—it was done. I had rejoined the 21st Century.

Cheryl was right; Facebook was exactly what I needed. As a stay at home caretaker, I hadn't thought much about the outside world; now, once again, I needed a bridge to normalcy, a way to get out of myself and back into the world. Facebook is a link to world-wide intimacy—I guess everyone (not just widows) could use a little more love these days.

I started out looking up my close friends in Florida and New York, only to find that a number of them (mostly those older than me) were not on Facebook. The ones that were, responded right away, and within a short period of time, I had quite a few "friends," mostly close buddies, augmented by alumni from the college where I had taught for three years and was planning to teach two courses in the fall.

I began branching out, going back a few years, and adding friends from previous jobs and different times in my life. It was great to touch base with these people, who all seemed so happy to hear from me. (Much happier, I believe, than if I'd sent them an email. Facebook still has a cache, even to the 22 year-old alumni; it's still considered the thing to do.)

One day, I stumbled upon my old hair stylist and astrologer from New York, a man I hadn't seen since 1990. I sent a friend request and heard back immediately: "Is this the Joanna who was so wonderful and funny and beautiful, and whom I loved so much?"

Now of course your hair stylist will always call you beautiful, even if he hasn't seen you for 20 years, but I was touched, and wrote back, thanking Chuck for his kind words and telling him about Jack. His response brought tears to my heart: "So sorry to hear of your loss, but life is large, it's all there, it just needs you to morph back into it, all new. xxxooo"

Something opened in my heart while reading this message. Yes, I thought, it was time to "morph" back into the world. It took an old friend I hadn't seen in two decades to tell me.

The following week, on the anniversary of the opening of "Please Stand By," the film that Jack and I had produced in the 1970s, I decided to reach out to some of the old cast and crew, many of whom I hadn't heard from in over 30 years. Here was my message:

"On this, the eve of the 39th anniversary of "Please Stand By," I thought I'd say hello, in remembrance of Jack, who died this year. Regards, Joanna." Not very warm and fuzzy, but accurate, right?

My first message and friend request went to Wendy in California, the star of our movie, whom I'd spoken with on the phone two years ago, and who knew about Jack's illness and passing. She responded almost immediately, confirming my friend request and sending a loving greeting. In an hour I'd sent my message to ten people, and had already heard back from four, including an email from Paula, an old friend in San Francisco, who'd been like family at one point. She and her boyfriend John, both in our movie, had been our closest friends in the early 70s, going to demonstrations, camping, and spending the night at each other's houses. When her email arrived, I was still busy sending out friend requests and remembrance messages, so I didn't look at it right away. When I finally did, an hour later, I was shocked—she told me that John had died of a heart attack a month and a half earlier. If I hadn't contacted Paula, I never would have known.

The confirmations continued into the night, along with messages: "Sorry to hear about Jack. How are you?" (from Paul, one of our cinematographers); "Sad news, but great to hear from you. Bronwyn and I are both well..." (from Arthur, the other cinematographer). However, I was still in a daze from the news of John's death. Then I found out that another old friend, Bob, the best man at our wedding, who was also in our movie, had died of a stroke just three weeks earlier.

Suddenly, it was all okay. I realized that Jack had his buddies with him now: John and Bob— good old friends. He was not alone; I didn't have to worry about him anymore.

I'm sure Facebook serves many purposes for many people, but for me that night, it brought healing on a whole new level.

Guidelines for Facebook

Just one—if you haven't yet joined, do so.

Chapter Twenty

You Will Make Mistakes

Don't be too hard on yourself. This is a time in your life when you're not the "you" you've grown accustomed to. No matter how together you think you are, there are probably large gaps in your thinking and feeling ability—gaps where you are protecting yourself against too much pain. So making important decisions in the early months of widowhood, as we've said, is a no-no.

That being said, if you do find yourself making an error in judgment, don't blame yourself too harshly. You are in mourning, even if you're not crying every minute. You are grieving for your loss, so if you make a mistake—well, what can you expect?

I myself made a couple of doozies. About four months into my widowhood, I decided I was handling it really well, and that I should get out and do something serious. One of the local museums had featured an Internet story of mine on its website the previous year—so I decided I'd volunteer to do public relations. I knew how to write press releases; I'd done PR before—what could go wrong?

Plenty, as it turned out. I should have realized I wasn't ready for this type of job, simply by the fact that I was unbelievably nervous walking up to the front door of the Museum. The director was out to lunch so I had to come back, and I almost didn't, but after an ice cream cone and a cup of coffee, I'd psyched myself up to try again.

This time, the director was in, and we had a very nice chat. Suzanne was charming and gracious, if not overly ecstatic about my offer, but she admitted she could use some help. I got the feeling she was being kind, having been told of my widowhood, and even though I think she'd have preferred my manning the cash register in the gift shop, she agreed to let me do publicity.

My first assignment was to write a promotional article on an upcoming exhibit, which would include an interview with a Board member. Here's where the problems began. I had an extraordinarily difficult time contacting the Board member, and when I finally did, she was rather nasty to me. Hurt, I retreated back into my shell, thinking someone should teach that woman how to treat volunteers.

Someone should, but evidently it wasn't going to be me. When I brought the article in on my next visit to the museum, Suzanne told me it would have to be approved by the Board member.

"Estelle has to okay everything around here," she murmured, not meeting my gaze.

I could tell the Suzanne wasn't wild about this rule, but evidently she was in no position to argue with it. So I emailed the article to Estelle, and after two weeks of gentle reminders, a nasty email came back, along with a completely butchered article. Estelle had taken it upon herself to interview another Board member (under my byline), and the result was a hodge podge.

Now, I've had lots of rejections in my life (all writers have), and usually I've taken them in stride, knowing it's part of the business. Not this time. I dissolved into tears, and cancelled my next museum visit—in fact, I did not return to the museum for two months. I emailed my notes to Suzanne with an apology, saying I'd fallen ill and was too sick to continue.

The problem was, I simply wasn't ready. I wasn't ready to plunge into the world of Museum publicity writing, no matter how good my intentions were. I'd worked at a Museum before, and was well aware of the difficulties one can face just writing a simple press release, but as a new widow, I didn't have my protective ego shield up. I was raw, hurting—and the experience made me hurt even more.

That being said, I'm still somewhat proud of myself for volunteering—I had never done anything like that before.

Equally as foolish, was my visit to the Veteran's Administration Center. Jack was a veteran, and I had been told that benefits were available if the veteran's service years fell within a certain range: the years an actual war was in progress. Jack had served in Korea, but it was during the Vietnam era, so I felt he might qualify.

I made two trips to DeLand and sent for Jack's army records, but to no avail—there was no record of his ever having been in Vietnam. Thus, he was not eligible for the "Agent Orange" compensation—which I could have gathered from the outset if I'd wanted to face the facts.

But perhaps I needed to acknowledge his service, since, for most of the time we were together, Jack and I were adamantly anti-war, and he didn't want much to do with the army. It was only in his later years, when he began to visit the VA hospital in Florida for treatment, that we—both of us—began to realize how important his service was in our lives.

Don't get mad at yourself for following a wild goose chase or dead end track—there may be some hidden meaning in it after all, such as an element that is part of the grieving process you are engaged in.

Guidelines for Handling Mistakes

1. Don't overestimate what you are capable of doing emotionally right now. For most people, mental

capacities far outstrip emotional stamina in any difficult situation. You may think you're ready to tackle an extra job, or even difficult household tasks, and mentally you are, but emotionally, you may find yourself unable to continue.

2. At the same time, don't get mad at yourself for volunteering for things you are ultimately unable to handle—you are a widow and entitled to change your mind.

3. If you do find yourself entangled in some situation of your own making, and you want out, get out! There's no law that says you're stuck with the predicament.

4. Don't let anybody push you into doing something you're not ready to do.

5. If you find yourself barking up the wrong tree, and have to back out, look for a little bit of *meaning* in the experience. Chances are you'll find it.

Chapter Twenty-One

Your Looks

In the first few months of your widowhood, how you look will probably be the last thing on your mind. That's okay—to a point. Most of us, by the time we hit 60, or even 55, have accepted how we look and don't worry much about it anymore. I remember looking in the mirror, and putting on makeup when I was down in Key Largo on my first grieving trip, and scarcely even "seeing" myself. After all, we've got a lot other things to attend to right now.

As I said, this is all okay—but there are limits. You don't want to "let yourself go." That's not good for you, and it's not necessary. So what can you do to maintain a nice appearance, even when the image in the mirror isn't someone you feel all that friendly toward?

I recommend clothes. Not just clothes—*fashion*. Even if your nose, chin, eyes and lips hold no interest for you at the moment, you might find that a soft, snuggly sweater in a pretty color can bring you happiness. A silk shirt can make you feel good; a long, swinging skirt can enliven your step. In short, paying attention to what you wear is a healthy preoccupation right now—not only is it one of the nurturing steps (that is, the *buying* of clothes), but it's also a sensual, physical indulgence. Clothes that fit our body are soothing; clothes in pretty colors can brighten our mood. Most of all, wearing an attractive outfit can tell you that you look good, and looking good is, well—nice.

Now, as everyone knows, in order to look good in clothes, we have to fit into them, right? Weight can be a problem for some new widows. Either we lose our appetites through grief and start to shed pounds without really wanting to, or we use food as a comfort tool and balloon up to be as much as 50 pounds overweight without noticing. Loss of appetite is serious. If it persists for any length of time, I suggest you see a therapist—it may be a sign of depression. Gaining weight, while also serious, can be managed during widowhood by the use of the "Leave 1/3 Diet."

This diet is good at any time, but particularly useful when you don't want to think too much about dieting. It works well when combined with a little exercise, like walking, and it is especially effective during hot weather, when most people don't want to eat that much anyway.

Start the Leave 1/3 Diet by going out to lunch—that's right, take yourself out for a solo lunch, as suggested in an earlier chapter, but don't go to a fancy restaurant, or one that is so fabulous you can't resist gobbling up everything on your plate. A good family restaurant works well; I usually start out at the IHop, and order a small steak. You have to get something substantial; starting the Leave 1/3 Diet on a shrimp cocktail is not going to work. So get a steak, roast turkey, or a plate of pasta, along with a salad, baked potato, vegetables, roll and butter, coffee, even dessert, and leave 1/3 of everything.

The waitress may ask you if you want a box: you say no. What you want is the experience of leaving food on your plate. Yes, this is hard—many of us will remember our mother's "think of the starving children in China" admonition, and that situation is probably still true. There are starving people all over the world, but you getting fat is not going to help them. (If you're really worried, send a donation to Unicef or

Save the Children; that will do more than your one-third of a baked potato.)

After a while, you'll get used to leaving 1/3 of the meal on your plate, and you can even take it home for later (just don't gobble it up in the car on the way.) It's easier leaving food on your plate at home, because you can always put it in a container and heat it up for lunch the next day. The hardest task (which is maybe not worth the difficulty) is leaving 1/3 on your plate when you're out to dinner at a friend or relative's house. I usually go off the diet in these instances.

The Leave 1/3 Diet will ensure that you fit into your clothes all during the first year of your widowhood, which means, as you begin to care about your looks again, you won't have any unpleasant surprises.

After all, everyone wants to look nice, even widows.

Guidelines for Dealing with Your Looks

1. Don't worry too much if you lose interest in your appearance for a while—it will come back.

2. If a serious situation starts to occur—severe weight loss, for example, or unexplained rashes or bumps— see a doctor.

3. Stay in control of your weight by whatever means necessary. (You can gage this easily by your ability to fit into your clothes.)

4. Buy yourself some treat to spark interest in your appearance—a new lipstick is good, as well as a beaded vest, a pretty shirt or a fabulous new handbag. (Did I mention shoes?)

5. Maintain hair care. If you dye your hair continue to do so. Continue getting haircuts, and of course, wash your hair as often as usual. If you can keep the hair and weight going, everything else will fall into place.

Chapter Twenty-Two

Dealing with Guilt

Guilt can creep up on you. You many not feel it at first. You're so busy trying to survive, trying to take care of yourself, your responsibilities, your job, and your family, but after a while, you may begin to notice a few twinges of a very uncomfortable sensation.

"If only I'd done such and such," you think—for example, made your husband get more exercise, eat less salt, or lower his cholesterol. Stop blaming yourself, dear widow. You aren't responsible for the when, the why or the how of your husband's death, no matter how much you think you are. You're not God. You weren't in charge of your husband's life. You were his wife, and as a wife, there was only so much you could do.

It's easy to play the blame game when a loved one is dead, and if there's no one else around to fit the bill, it's even easier to blame yourself. Many women lose sleep over this. One widow told me she was afraid she'd be arrested any moment for causing her husband's death, because she let him eat too many sweets.

Another friend, whom we'll call Susan, had an even more severe accusation to bludgeon herself with: "My husband was in so much pain during the last stages of his cancer," she told me. "He'd beg me for more pain killers. Maybe he took some extra when I was out shopping; I just don't know."

If your husband has been sick for a while, you know what an agonizing experience it can be—watching someone you love in great stress. You try and stay ready for anything, but after several nights without sleep, it's hard, sometimes, to be totally on top of things. Many people have help at this time: Hospice, or home health care, maybe even a full-time nurse.

Some men only want their wives around to take care of them. You become nurse, cook, companion, psychiatrist and much more—for months on end. This is called "caretaking," and it can be grueling. The stress can last long after your loved one's death, surfacing as "guilt" that you didn't do everything perfectly.

Then suddenly, it's over. The focus of all the loving attention has been taken away, leaving you empty.

As time goes by, you wish your husband was still with you. The agony of caretaking has subsided, and only the bittersweet memory remains. Oh! If only he were here! Oh, if only you hadn't fallen asleep that afternoon (or run out to the store, or talked to a friend on the phone). This is grief—and it's pretty unpleasant.

My own experience is a case in point. Jack had been sick for five years, but was still able to function pretty well until the last month. Suddenly, he seemed to plunge downhill rapidly. After a week in the hospital, he was told to get Hospice, or a home health care nurse. He chose the latter.

Guilt Point #1: Would he have done better with Hospice? Should I have tried to talk him into it? Two days after his release from the hospital he was back in the ER—the home health care nurse had said his blood pressure was way too low. When we got there, we were told this was a mistake—Jack's blood pressure was okay. So we went home.

Guilt Point #2: Should I have insisted upon a more thorough examination? Jack died the next day.

These questions plagued me for months. You see how you can beat yourself up about this, and believe me, I did. If you're prone to guilt, as some people are, it can take quite a while to really handle this. In fact, guilt is a major reason why people go into therapy—that, and anger that your loved one is no longer with you. A therapist will tell you, no, it wasn't your fault that your husband died. A therapist will tell you it's normal to be angry at your husband for dying and leaving you.

Guilt can persist on and on in subtle forms. For instance, you may find yourself experiencing anxiety months after your husband passed, for no explainable reason, or you'll see something—someone wearing a shirt like one your husband owned, or a sign on a billboard for a restaurant the two of you liked—and you'll burst into tears. You've been coping just fine, but you miss him. You're still grieving. Then it starts: Oh, if only I'd given him more compliments when he was alive!

We can never really go back and fix whatever it was we wished we'd handled better, but we can know that our husband appreciated all our caretaking, and all the love we bestowed upon him. Of course he did, and not even guilt can take that away.

Guidelines for Handling Guilt

1. If you are unable to sleep for weeks on end, or if you've lost your appetite and have no interest in doing anything, you may be struggling with a depression caused by guilt. The best thing for you to do is to see a therapist.

2. If your guilt is intermittent—it comes and goes, know that eventually it will subside. It's inevitable that you will have a little bit of guilt when your husband dies— for no other reason than you're still here and he isn't.

3. Try to maintain a rational approach to the guilt. What seems overwhelming and terrible at 3 a.m., can be viewed much more dispassionately at 12 noon the next day. No, your mother's birthday gift didn't cause his heart attack, even if it was the ugliest sweater you'd ever seen.

4. Be gentle with yourself in dealing with guilt. If anxiety arises, stick to your tried and true measures—a decaf cappuccino and a cherry pastry at Panera will do wonders for an anxiety attack.

5. Know that pain, grieving, and mourning your loved one is not guilt. Don't stop the grieving process before you are ready.

Chapter Twenty-Three

Money

Considering how important money is in all of our lives, it may seem odd that I have left mention of it until Chapter 23. That may shed light on how much more important *other* things seem to the new widow (or at least how they did to me).

I am not rich. I've had a full-time job most of my life. In 2009, Jack and I sold a piece of land in upstate New York, which enabled me to retire from my college teaching job and take care of him. I will never regret that decision, even though it left me a bit up in the air, career-wise.

I knew the proceeds from the land sale, plus my slim savings, would not last very long. So, after Jack's death, I created a budget of sorts and set about restricting my expenditures. I've never been very good at this. My philosophy tends to veer toward the spiritual, "consider the lilies of the field," orientation:

"Therefore, take no thought saying, what shall we eat, or what shall we drink? Or wherefore shall we be clothed?...For your heavenly Father knoweth that ye have need of all these things."

-Matthew 6:31-32

I can't say these ideas have always worked for me, or that I never had a sleepless night worrying about money. (I've had sleepless nights worrying about everything since I've been a widow; money is no exception.) Perhaps because I had a little bit of savings, and a little bit of social security, plus the promise of two courses to teach at my old college in the fall, I was not consumed with money worries.

I tried, every month, to pay most of my household bills from social security. Then, for additional expenses, such as clothes or little trips, I'd use my savings. I figured that now was the time I needed this money. I remember my parents' conversation, back in 1984, after my dad's first heart attack: my mother didn't want to break into the emergency cash, until my father reassured her, "Becky, Becky, this *is* an emergency!"

So I considered that it was okay to use some of my savings in order to nurture myself back to emotional health. I didn't go crazy; I had a limit on what I'd spend going out to lunch (about $15-$20) and dinner ($20-$35). I used coupons from Coldwater Creek for most of my clothes shopping. (I believe I mentioned how important shopping was in my recovery.)

My biggest splurge was little trips—yet I believe these solo excursions played a huge part in nursing me back to health. My first trip to Key Largo, where I stayed at the Marriott for two nights, cost about $500, not including gas. The second trip, to a very classy place in Jupiter, Florida called the Jupiter Beach Resort, was a bit more, about $650. At both of these hotels, I indulged in room service—but I brought my own bottle of wine.

My monthly household budget is probably typical, running something like this:

```
Electricity........... $125
Water .................. $75
Gas heating........ $35 (higher in winter)
Car insurance.... $65
Dish TV.............. $58
Internet .............. $20
```

Phone..................$85
YMCA $35
Daily expenses .. $300

Of course, I usually went over the daily expense budget, especially as gas began to soar, but I rationalized; I'd have a part-time job in the fall; *now* was the time I needed solace.

I was fortunate that Jack and I had paid off our mortgage in 2002, and I'd paid off the balance of my car loan from the profits of the land sale. But I still had some credit card debt, and lots of repairs needed for the house. I could have done a lot of worrying about money, if I'd wanted to. I just chose not to, and for that I am thankful.

In the early 1990s, enjoying a brief period of an inheritance, I opened a real estate/art gallery business in Florida. The art gallery made very little money, the real estate not much more—but it was a time in my life when I felt rather wealthy. My real estate partner and I used to drive around giving out boxes of food to homeless people in the street, boxes complete with can openers and eating utensils. We did this for a couple of years, and it always felt gratifying. Whether it's instant karma, God, or just plain good luck, I feel like someone is giving me boxes of food now—that is, my material needs are being met.

I wish the same for you, dear widow.

Guidelines for Thinking About Money

1. Do not make any important changes in your overall situation, such as selling your house, simply because you are worried about money at the moment. Remember, as a new widow, reality can be a bit distorted—your status may not be as bad as you think.

2. On the other hand, if you know things are going to be tight, make yourself a little budget, and try to stick

to it until you feel comfortable making any necessary changes.

3. Entertain the possibility of a part-time job. It's amazing how doing just a small amount of paid work can improve your view of your finances.

4. You can economize in ways that are not particularly painful—using coupons, for instance, for everything from clothes to sugar.

5. I'll go out on a limb and suggest using a bit of your nest egg for self-nourishment—a little vacation, for instance, or some new clothes. After all, what you are going through now is considered to be one of the most stressful periods in anyone's life.

Chapter Twenty-Four

Find a Project

After five or six months of coping with it all, you may decide you need something to sink your teeth into, especially if you don't have a job. (If you do have a job, you may need a diversion as well—jobs at this time can be difficult.) What you need is something you love, but also an endeavor that doesn't require an overwhelming amount of time or responsibility on your part. You need a *project*.

A project is some activity that commands your complete attention, but doesn't keep you up nights worrying about deadlines or quotas or assessments—terms usually associated with a job. At the same time, your activity must be engaging enough that it takes your mind off your loss, your loneliness, and your feeling of rattling around the house in a vacuum (or rattling around your job in a daze, which can also occur).

A worthwhile project can meet both these requirements. Typically, a project will be something for which you are primarily responsible—although a friend or relative may be involved. My project came by way of a friend. Karen, another writer, had completed the first draft of a book, which she asked me to edit. Her manuscript was thrilling: an autobiographical journey through the alternative spiritual paths of our time: reiki, reincarnation, angels and other mystical helpmates. I would have edited such a manuscript for free, but Karen insisted on paying me (and it felt good to make a little money after a year and a half of retirement).

Karen's story took her from Virginia to Egypt, to study the Great Pyramids, and to France, in search for the tomb of Mary Magdalene. She discussed extra terrestrials, past life regression, and the phenomenon of Stonehenge from a first-hand perspective. To say this project was diverting would be an understatement. It occupied all my waking thoughts for a while—yet, because Karen and I were friends, there was no pressure or discomfort of any kind. It was the perfect project.

My editing work on Karen's book lasted three months, and when I was finished, I was a different person. I had gone through an "experience" different from my experience of mourning, and come out on the other side. It was the first step in my healing.

We all have things we love to do that can be turned into a captivating project with faith and a little bit of optimism. How do we find a project that is right for us, without over-stepping our capabilities? The truth, I think, is to let the project find you. When something lands on your doorstep, seems to beckon to you, and you *anticipate* doing it, chances are the project is right for you. (This is different than de-ciding, perhaps too early on, to take on the responsibility of a free-lance job or a stressful volunteer activity, such as I did in volunteering to do publicity at a museum.) A worth-while project will cause minimum stress. It won't keep you up nights or cause friction with other people. A worthwhile project will be marked by your enthusiasm, your delight and the lack of obstacles in your participation. In short, a worth-while project will be marked with *love*.

So keep your eyes open, dear widow. That cherished activity is just around the corner, waiting for you. When it comes, you'll know it by the good feeling in your heart.

Guidelines for Finding a Project

1. The worthwhile project will probably make its way into your life after five or six months of widowhood. If your choice turns out to be "a mistake," don't worry. Another project will pop up soon!

2. The worthwhile project will be characterized by your enthusiasm and feeling of confidence that you can do it. You can.

3. The worthwhile project will probably involve something already close to your heart. If you like to draw, maybe a friend will be looking for an artist to do portraits at a local street fair. Don't be shy! Or maybe there's an opportunity to organize a community garden in your neighborhood, and gardening is "your thing." Go for it, dear!

4. The worthwhile project, although it may be solo, might entail your involvement with others in a harmonious relationship. It is a chance to restore the balance between you and the outside world, which needs to happen at every moment possible.

5. Enjoy your project. It will lead you toward the doorway of the new you.

Part Three:
Learning to Enjoy Life Again

Chapter Twenty-Five

Healing

I am at Canaveral Seashore National Park, on the beach, looking at waves and feeling the sun, but I'm also feeling a cool breeze, refreshing as the ice water I have at my elbow.

Yes, it is peaceful. I'm not totally alone—an elderly couple is sitting under an umbrella some ways away, and I'm grateful for that. I'm not sure I'd want to be out here completely alone.

As it is, I am as alone right now as I've ever been in my life; no husband, no parents, a brother 3000 miles away. I have friends, yes, plenty of them—but not here with me now. Yet, I do not feel alone, or even lonesome. I feel like I have *myself*. I know who I am—I'm a widow, of six and one-half months, who has begun to feel herself healed. The guilt is gone (largely, or at least, right at this moment). The fear of being alone is definitely gone. I can stay by myself in the house for hours on end—Saturday night, Sunday afternoon, any day of the week. I am not afraid.

There is something beautiful and natural about being alone. We are, after all, singular creatures—we are not born in pairs. (Most of us aren't; there are exceptions.) We go to school, interact with others, love, and marry—all as individual people. Often, in marriage, we lose part of our individuality. If we are lucky, we don't lose too much. If our spouse is enlightened, he helps us hold onto *who we are*.

Now, as a widow, we come, once again, face to face with that person. Old cares drop away as we slowly emerge from our grief. We no longer have another *person* to look after. If that loved one was sick for a number of years, we may find ourselves surprised at this "self" that is emerging. This self is so much less anxious than the self we've come to know. Taking care of a husband, no matter how dear, does cause a bit of anxiety. We never feel quite at ease.

Even if your husband wasn't ill, and even if your loved one's death was sudden, there is going to come a day when you look around and realize you don't have to be anywhere else than where you are right now. You don't have to do anything else than what you choose to do at this particular moment. Conditioned as we are to "the other," that realization may, at first, bring a tremor of its own: what are you *doing* here?

What are you doing here? You are walking the path to recovery. You are being *healed*.

The sun is beginning to sink now, and the light over the ocean is beautiful. I can't see the sunset here—I'm on the ocean side—but I know when I walk over the little wooden bridge toward the river, I'll see it. I'll be doing that very soon.

Our recovery is a bit like that—we can't quite see that dazzle of color that we know is us—not quite yet, but the inner light is changing. We can feel something new and different emerging. We know that eventually we're going to walk over that bridge into a new and glorious *self.*

Guidelines for Healing

1. Look for ways to express yourself, so that you can see and feel the "you" that is emerging.

2. There's no need to rush any of this, but when you do feel it, don't close the door on these new emotions. They are the beginning of healing.

3. Engage in alone time; don't fear it. It is when you are alone that you are most likely to discover the real you.

4. Seek activities that allow you an opportunity to get to know yourself: taking walks, indulging in short car trips, or writing in your journal (or computer) in the park.

5. When you feel the door open to a new discovery, embrace it, write it down, and above all, don't feel guilty with your new find. Remember, your husband wants you to be healed.

Chapter Twenty-Six

Maybe a Job...

The day I went back to work was a nervous one indeed. I set two alarm clocks, not trusting either one to wake me at 6:30 a.m. I needn't have worried, because I woke at 6, groggy, but ready to go. Today was the Fall Orientation meeting, where the faculty at the college where I'd be teaching two classes met to discuss the goals for the year.

I felt a little reluctant getting out of bed—my one and one-half year vacation from the world of work was now officially over. For a moment, I wanted to crawl back into bed and pull the covers over my head. I was scared: could I do it? Could I face some 20-odd students three days a week and tell them what I knew about magazine writing and news editing? At that moment, I wasn't sure.

I took a moment to glance at my husband's photo in the commemorative bookmark, given to me by Michelle after the memorial service. Jack was always supportive of my teaching. "I don't know how you do it every day," he used to say when I taught full-time. "It was all I could do to teach one class, and I was in my 30s!"

Jack had conducted a film class at the School of Visual Arts in New York in the 1970s, and I'd taught two courses at Hunter College, but hadn't started teaching full-time until 2000. Actually, as teachers know, you get into a rhythm when you're teaching, and full-time isn't that different than adjunct teaching, as far as the classes go. It's the paperwork that kills you with full-time teaching—that, and the meetings. Now, with just two courses, I wouldn't have that much paperwork, and wouldn't be attending meetings.

I got dressed, ate a boiled egg and some toast, and drove off to school, just like in the old days. On the way to school, I felt a strange burst of exhilaration: I was doing it; I was going to a job. I knew Jack would be proud of me. It felt suddenly comfortable, being dressed up for work and driving a car—I had rejoined the human race.

The Orientation Meeting was predictable, and at noon I came home for lunch—there was another meeting at 2 p.m. I ate my hamburger slowly, wishing I didn't have to go back. I didn't really feel part of things as an adjunct, but at the moment, that's all I'd been offered, and it was certainly all I thought I could handle.

The 2 p.m. meeting for the faculty of the School of Arts and Humanities was friendly and comforting. I was welcomed back as part of the family, and greeted several colleagues I'd been close to as a full-time teacher. My department head had mentioned earlier that one of the new faculty hires hadn't shown up—after the meeting she asked if she could talk to me. I wondered what was up.

Dr. Walker gave me the keys to her office since she had to talk to the Dean first, and while waiting in her office I prayed, fervently, that any decision I made would be the right one. Was Dr. Walker going to offer me a full-time position? If so, could I handle it? I'd been out of the classroom a year and half—did I even have the physical stamina to teach full-time now? Department meetings, advising, grading papers— teaching full-time in any college is highly demanding, and I'd been so protected of late.

Dr. Walker came back, and we began to talk; in less than 10 minutes she'd offered me the full-time position, and I'd accepted. I'd be teaching public relations, different than journalism, but maybe, I reasoned, a bit more fun? I felt an excitement growing as we talked about the job. I'd served as a PR director for three years in New York and certainly knew the ropes. Dr. Walker was expressing such confidence in me, I could hardly say no. My spirits kept rising. As a PR instructor I'd be going to luncheons. I'd need some new clothes...

I left Dr. Walker's office after two hours of chatting, convinced I could do the job. In fact, I felt less nervous contemplating my full-time position than I had thinking about my adjunct job. Were my worries unfounded in the first place?

While I've been cautioning you, dear widow, on almost every page, to keep nurturing yourself and provide extra pampering for your wounded heart, there's going to come a day when you're ready to step out into the world. With some widows this happens very quickly: Janine, one of the other funeral directors working with Michelle, went back to her job in eight weeks. I wasn't ready to teach for seven months, but when offered the chance for a new position with greater responsibility, I found I was ready. I'd done lots of healing those seven months, and evidently, I was more eager to work than I thought I was.

Don't sell yourself short. While the human heart may take months, even years to recover, your brain and intellect might be dying for a challenge. As I've mentioned, mental capacities heal more quickly than emotions—your mind may be itching to get back into the harness.

If you're offered a challenge on the job during your widowhood, it probably means you can do it.

Guidelines for Going Back to Work

6. Don't underestimate your work capacity. Just because your emotions are still healing, that doesn't mean you should sit home and stew—a job may be exactly what you need.

7. On the other hand, don't rush back to work too soon. If you feel panic or nauseated at the thought of a job, it's way too early.

8. Be frank with your employers about your mental and emotional state. If you're feeling unsure, ask a close friend for a second opinion on your work readiness.

9. Trust your instincts! If the thought of a particular job brings a ripple of excitement to your mind, go for it.

10. Be aware of serendipity—if a job seems to "fall into your lap," and you like the idea, chances are that opportunity is right for you.

Chapter Twenty-Seven

Memories

In the first few months of your widowhood, remembering things you did with your husband, places you went, and "moments" you shared, can be quite painful. You may feel yourself turning away from the memory with a start, almost as if you'd been bitten by a mosquito. Ouch, that hurts!

After a while, though, the quality of this experience will probably start to change. You may find yourself thinking rather longingly of the past, and then you may even begin to linger in those memories. It's when you begin to daydream about the past, and then leap into a fantasy about the future, that you'll probably say, "I'm beginning to feel like myself again."

My friend Marie, who's been a widow about five years, has a good rationale for memories. "Our husband lives on in those thoughts," she says. "It's a way for us to stay in touch with what we loved about him."

It's true for many widows that, as time passes, the memories grow sweeter. We forget or disregard those matrimonial quarrels (What? Argue? We never argued!) and we tend to settle into a warm, fuzzy blanket of happy recollections.

That's called *comfort*. If we remembered every single tiff and spat with everyone in our lives, our mind would become a rather unpleasant place to visit. So we don't, and we definitely don't linger there when we reminisce about times with our dear husband.

The problem is, the rosy glow, cozy as it can become, is a somewhat unrealistic situation, and even a barrier to our healing. We don't want to stay "stuck" in love with our dead spouse. Of course we love him, we'll always love him, but if we allow our memories to build the man into the most perfect human being that ever lived, we're not going to do much else, other than lie around and wish he were here.

So memories can be a tough thing to deal with. On the one hand, if they're sweet, we want to indulge them. On the other, if we start to compare everyday reality with the memory of our husband and our time with him, we can actually block our own growth and development.

Because, ladies, we are still growing. Just because we're widows does not mean we are dead. It's important to keep growing, changing, and learning about ourselves. Our generation, the baby boomers, was all about self-discovery—we certainly don't want to stop now.

As I write this, I'm sitting in a booth at the Olive Garden, about three blocks from the university where I taught for three years. It's also right across the street from Halifax Hospital, where Jack spent the last full week of his life. (He was at home two days before he died, then back at Halifax.) During his hospital stay, I came to the Olive Garden twice for dinner—alone, tearful, and comforted greatly by a compassionate waitress. That week, when I knew my husband was dying, was also one of the times when I loved him most. I was frantically in love with Jack toward the end, and he with me—we hadn't had such a perfect rapport since our first honeymoon in 1969. It's tempting to stay there, at that point of togetherness, joined in love and pain forever more. (As I write this, I'm still wearing my wedding ring, but the other day I took it off, and moved it to the right hand, just to see how it felt.)

Wearing my wedding ring reminds me of where we bought it—in Key West, just before our second marriage ceremony. It also reminds me of our first wedding in 1969 in New York City. Both times, I experienced that special glow one feels from getting married, that delicious feeling of gentle possessiveness, accompanied by the "high" of joining one's future to another's.

While the "high" of getting married may not last too long—six months is typical—the love and strength we've received from sharing a life with a husband does—on and on, maybe into eternity.

No, I'm not ready to give up that memory of my husband's last week with me. I realize that during those days he knew how much I loved him, and that means a lot. But someday I will relinquish it—and the wedding ring—and put them on the other hand, the less significant hand.

Guidelines for Memories

1. Try to be realistic about your memories. Don't build your husband into a paragon of virtue that no one else can ever measure up to.

2. At the same time, let your heart be soothed by pleasant memories. Realize they are something to be grateful for.

3. As your memories move from painful to bittersweet to affectionate recollections, acknowledge to yourself that you are healing.

4. Talk and write about memories of your husband with people who knew him.

5. Take a "memory reminder" with you as you are lunching out, going on vacation or just visiting the park: a photo, a ring, or a gift that he gave you. You will be soothed.

Chapter Twenty-Eight

Sexual Fantasies

When a male colleague at the college where I worked invited me to go out one Friday night I wasn't really surprised, because I'd known the guy several years. But I thought it was too soon, and so I said no. (Plus I had other plans so I couldn't have gone even if I wanted to.) However, I was flattered, and on the way to my rendezvous with the girls I preened my feathers a bit, glad I was still attractive to *someone*.

Late that night, going to bed, I thought again about the invitation and wondered, if I were to start going out with the guy, if he'd eventually want to have sex. I was looking at my husband's picture on the laminated bookmark I use in my journal, and so I asked him, "What do you think, Jack?" I could almost swear he winked at me (of course I know he didn't), but even more amazing was the voice I heard in my head—Jack's voice.

"Can I watch?" he said mischievously.

Hearing that, and looking at Jack's face in the photo, I felt a wave of sexual desire sweep over me. My husband and I had been good with sex; in fact, ill as he was, Jack and I had indulged in some kind of sexual activity right up to about six weeks before he passed away. But—

"Can I watch?"

The idea of my husband watching me and another man turned me on, and I couldn't stop thinking about it. I'd had several sexual fantasies since he'd passed away, but they'd been lukewarm, until now. Now I had to do something about it, and you can probably guess what I did.

Masturbation has gone out of style in recent decades (at least as a topic to write about; I doubt if the practice itself has decreased in popularity). When I wrote for *Cosmopolitan* in the 1970s and 80s, I often referred to masturbation in the course of an article as I gave advice to women on one topic or another. It was part of women's empowerment in those days, but the last time I've heard masturbation mentioned was by Kim Catrell in "Sex in the City," over 10 years ago.

As a widow, suddenly bereft of sexual intimacy, you may want to try this, especially if you're not interested in an actual partner at the moment—or ever. There is no age limit to sexual fantasies and their gratification. My mother, widowed at 75, reported having juicy fantasies almost nightly for a while. She was pretty amazed, but I wasn't; the female libido can persevere long past menopause if we want it to.

So don't be surprised if you find yourself having erotic dreams as early as two to four months after your husband's death, especially if the two of you were sexually active. My first erotic dream concerned an old boyfriend from college, but my husband was in there someplace. I couldn't remember much of what had gone on by the time I woke up, but I did remember the warm sexy feeling that is so delightful—it lingered with me as I started my day.

But I never sought out a sex fantasy during my first six months of widowhood—I was way too busy just trying to keep my head on straight. If I had an erotic dream I enjoyed it, but solo sex experiences, I felt were pretty much a thing of the past.

…Until the night that man asked me out, and I heard my husband's voice:

"Can I watch?"

Guidelines for Sexual Fantasies

1. I don't care who you are, or how old you are—you're probably going to have an erotic dream or sexual fantasy the first year of your widowhood. Enjoy it, dear.

2. On the other hand, you probably don't need to spend time seeking them out. For one thing, it may not work—I tried reading Anais Nin's *Delta of Venus* one lonely night, and nothing happened. You might be better off watching "Masterpiece Theater" on PBS and getting some Victorian titillation.

3. Don't hook up with some man you don't even know just because you miss having sex—that's what masturbation is for. (I gave the same advice to 30 year-olds in *Cosmopolitan* back in the 80s.)

4. If you are really craving sex, and can't seem to stimulate yourself, try watching any movie with Richard Gere. He seems to do it for us older gals.

5. Be kind to yourself. Sex is natural and healthy, and just because you're a widow doesn't mean you shouldn't have sex urges. Be an adult. Respect your husband's memory (maybe he'll be watching...you never know).

iPhone

I admit I've never been very technologically inclined, but the cell phone I'd been using since 2005 was a dinosaur, so when it stopped working completely in October, I decided to join three-fourths of my students and get an iphone. Several of my friends had recommended the iphone 4—I was due an upgrade, and when I walked into the ATT store it seemed natural to ask for one. The iphone 4S had come out two days earlier, so I got the regular iphone 4 at a good price.

That night I met my friend Anne for dinner—she was one of those who'd been recommending the iphone 4. All through our meal we played with our phones, feeling like 20-year olds. The next week, I joined my students in turning on my phone in between classes, checking emails, texting, and looking up info on the web. What fun! My phone was pretty, too—it had the sweetest little case with pink birds on it, and featured a pink rose as my screen saver.

All went well until the following weekend when, having a bit of free time on Sunday, I decided to try a few applications on my phone. First came a flashlight—free, and easy to install—voila! Now I'd be able to read menus in dark restaurants without the aid of my glasses. (Anne had shown me this little feat the week before.) I added Facebook, also easy to do, and then went on to Pandora, the Internet radio. I had no problem getting the account started; when asked for my favorite artist, I automatically typed in "Beatles." (Who else would an aging baby boomer start with? Well... maybe the Stones.)

The first song, "Hey, Jude," brought tears to my eyes. I thought of Jack, of course, and my first apartment on 14th Street in Manhattan, where Jack and I had met. How wonderful to be able to play the Beatles whenever I wanted! I was grateful for my new phone and for Pandora.

As "Hey, Jude" came to an end, I settled back on the couch, preparing to take a little nap, but to my surprise, another song began, this time "Band on the Run" by Wings. Hmmm. I picked up the phone and fiddled with it a while, trying to turn it off. It wouldn't turn off. I touched one button, which opened to give me a two-page biography of Paul McCartney—yes, I loved Paul, but maybe not right now.

"Band on the Run" ended, and "Imagine" started playing. I became a bit anxious—why couldn't I get Pandora to turn off? Would I have to walk into school the next day, "Sergeant Pepper" blaring from my purse, explaining my old-lady inability to turn off my cell phone radio?

No! Determined, I called the ATT store. All representatives were busy. It was a weekend, after all—the place had been packed the day I'd purchased my phone. I called the ATT tech number and reached a nice lady who, unfortunately, didn't know a whole lot about Pandora. She did, however, give me some valuable information on my new plan, including the fact that I was paying for Pandora, which had now been playing for about an hour. She also emailed me several tutorials. (Perhaps I should have read a tutorial to begin with?)

Hanging up, I squirmed a little as the picture of my embarrassment at school was now joined by the thought of a high cell phone bill for 24 hours of oldie-goldies. By this time, the Beatles had been replaced by the Mamas and Papas, Crosby, Stills & Nash, and yes, the Stones—a whole 60s repertoire of wonderful music, but right now, all I wanted was to turn the darn thing off.

Maybe that's why it's called Pandora? I thought, grabbing my handbag and running out to the car—because you don't know what you're getting yourself into?

On the way to the ATT store, I enjoyed "California Dreamin'" for the second time (was it making a loop?) and some great songs by Simon & Garfunkel, Jefferson Airplane, and the Grateful Dead. Those were the days! Oh, how I missed my hubby!

At the store, I was a bit embarrassed to walk in with Creedence Clearwater blasting "Full Moon Rising" from my phone, so I waited for a break between songs before entering. A nice 20-something representative turned Pandora off right away and showed me how to do it. She was very sweet, didn't smirk or even look the least bit condescending—maybe she was used to us oldsters and our fumbling fingers.

Then I went to Cold Stone Creamery and got an ice cream cone. That's something us baby boomers can take care of efficiently. For the rest of the afternoon I played with my new phone, trying out every application I could lay my hands on.

Guidelines for the iPhone

Just this—by all means, get one. It'll make you feel 20 years younger.

Chapter Thirty

Your Health

"What's this?" you think, as you wake up with what appears to be another weird ailment. First it was hives, then a strange lump on your arm (which went away after a week), and now your lip is swollen all out of proportion.

"It's allergy season," you say, searching for some antihistamine. The swelling goes down after a cup of coffee, however, making the antihistamine unnecessary. Thankfully, you apply lipstick, noting that the color on your mouth helps to diminish the appearance of a fat lip.

Relax, dear widow. Unexplained, even bizarre ailments are not unusual in your condition. A recent widow of my acquaintance who was usually in the peak of health reported the following symptoms during the first 10 weeks of widowhood: sinus headache, runny nose, discoloration of her hands, foot cramps, itchy elbow, restless leg syndrome, chronic indigestion, pink eye, spots on her neck, hair loss, and back pain. Fortunately, the woman also possessed a good sense of humor, and she began to see a pattern in the "illnesses"—they'd usually occur when she didn't want to do something, such as clean out her husband's closet. So instead of running to the doctor every time, she'd lie down and meditate for 45 minutes. Usually the symptoms would subside—or at least her fear of sickness would go away. Typically, the illness would be gone the next day.

Psychosomatic? Perhaps. Or maybe the state of grieving we're in calls for a little more coddling than we're used to giving ourselves.

Another widow, Janice, described how she went through a series of "mirroring" illnesses—that is, she experienced the same symptoms her husband had exhibited the last months of his illness. "Phil died of a heart attack," she told me, "and for three months I had intermittent chest pains. I went to a doctor but he said I was fine."

I had some of this mirroring effect myself. Jack had been diagnosed with COPD (chronic obstructive pulmonary disease) in addition to congestive heart failure; for the last six months of his life he relied on oxygen tanks. Unlike my husband, I had never smoked cigarettes, but it didn't take me long to experience breathing problems very similar to Jack's. No, I didn't resort to oxygen tanks, but I did clean the air conditioning ducts and worry about my condition for several months—before I realized I was okay.

If you find yourself suddenly consumed with attacks on your health, or experiencing highly unpleasant symptoms, such as nausea, cramping, dizziness or inability to walk, you may want to consult a therapist as well as a doctor. Grief may be stalking you in the form of a physical ailment. This is one visitor in your recovery process you definitely do not want to "be nice to."

Guidelines for Handling Your Health

1. Don't be surprised if you experience unusual, even bizarre health symptoms, unconnected to any you've had before.

2. Try to maintain a sense of perspective about your health—if your ailment seems serious, see a doctor, but if you know, deep in your heart, that it's stress related, don't go into a frenzy worrying about it.

3. Try meditation to relieve stress and get a sense of peace about your body and your mind.

4. Follow your typical diet and exercise routines to maintain health.

5. Keep a sense of humor about the whole situation—it will work wonders!

Chapter Thirty-One

Meditation

For those who don't know about meditation, it's value may come as rather a surprise. Meditation is good for the nerves, the back, blood pressure and the stomach. It can make us look at the world differently, and it can make *us* look better. Meditation is great for dealing with grief.

I first began practicing meditation about 10 years ago when I noticed a tendency to become light-headed during exercise. Hoping meditation might help this condition, I attended an introductory seminar on Transcendental Meditation at the Unity Church in my area. Transcendental Meditation, I learned, is meditation using a *mantra*—a word or phrase that is repeated or chanted until the mind is lulled and the awareness of "all" or "omnipotence" washes over us like waves on a beach. Since the actual Transcendental Meditation workshop, where participants are given personal mantras, costs over $1000, I decided to use the old standard, "Om mani padme hum," as my mantra. It worked then, free of charge, and it's been working ever since.

Once you have achieved a state of relative calm using your mantra, you can lie back and observe your breathing—in, out, in, out—or you can become aware of some lovely purple waves of energy in your mind's eye, which feel awfully good. In my friend Karen's book, *Rise and Shine*, which I edited over the summer, I learned that these purple or lavender waves of energy are associated with the Age of Aquarius—a concept that most of us baby boomers have at least heard of.

I've been told that the vibrations from chanting open the blood vessels and bring more oxygen to the body—I have not checked this out medically. I do know that after meditation I can look in the mirror and it seems as if there isn't a wrinkle on my face. That alone is good for the grieving process, where so much of our healing is connected with self-esteem.

The real value of meditation is what it is doing to the emotions. If we are sad or feeling lonesome for hubby, a half-hour mediation can replace those feeling with a sense of tranquility. Forty-five minutes of meditation can connect you with your past, present and future, and can allow you to feel one with your husband in a way that isn't scary or gloomy or super-syrupy. This is not a mental awareness—it's more of an all-over realization of the perfection of life. There are actually no words to describe it, other than saying it's very, *very* pleasant.

An hour's meditation—well, you get the picture.

Guidelines for Meditation

1. Lie down on your bed, a couch or the floor, with your legs slightly apart and your arms at your sides. You can have music on if you want to, but you don't have to. Meditation works just as well without music.

2. Close your eyes and begin to breathe in through your nose, and out through your mouth. Once comfortable, breath normally, taking slow, deep breaths.

3. If you like, begin to chant silently in your mind using a mantra. (You can do research on the Internet to find one of your own.) As mentioned, the time-honored "Om mani padme hum" works very well.

4. If you don't feel comfortable chanting, merely focus your attention on your breathing. When your mind

wanders, gently pull it back to your breathing. After a while this will become easier.

5.   Allow whatever feelings rise to surface, but try not to *think*. If thoughts intrude, go back to watching your breathing. It may take 20 or 30 minutes for a feeling of well-being to begin to manifest, but if you are patient, it will. (You may need several sessions just to make it to 20 or 30 minutes of meditation. Yes, the practice is hard, but each time you do it, meditation gets easier. Don't give up!)

Chapter Thirty-Two

Confidence

It can be hard to recover your confidence after bereavement. You might find yourself, as time progresses, exercising more caution than you typically would in going about your daily tasks. While caution is good, you may want to examine the motivation behind your unusual lack of spontaneity.

When someone we are close to dies, the standard atavistic reaction is, "How does this affect me?" We can't help this: we are human, and necessarily concerned about our own well-being, and that of our children. When your husband dies, no such question arises. The death of one's husband is so all-encompassing that we cannot capsulate our concern in terms of "affect."

Like it or not, you have probably created a co-dependency with your husband—most couples do. Co-dependency means that whatever he feels, you feel; what happens to him, happens to *you*. If you're lucky, you've also seen to it that certain aspects of your life have been reserved for you alone. Maybe you have a stimulating job that takes a lot of your attention; maybe you spend hours with a fulfilling hobby, or have a volunteer "cause" that occupies your time. Maybe you've saved a corner of your life to nurture artistic talents—painting, pottery, or poetry writing.

Whatever aspect of your life has rewarded you with *confidence* in yourself and your abilities should now be given a high priority. Because, unfortunately, when our husband dies, we may feel as if a part of us has died too. So we need *resuscitation* in a big way.

Look for activities that give your self-esteem a boost. If your job makes you feel empowered, give it all you've got. When a co-worker praised my efforts in a group email, I was more than typically pleased—I was *revived*. (No, I am not dead, I thought to myself. I can still perform my job duties well enough to be praised.)

Conversely, if your job is not giving you enough of an ego boost, you may want to think about changing it—you need all the praise you can get right now. Look for ways to build your own confidence. If you can paint well, then paint. If you're good at fundraising for your church, get out and fundraise. If cooking is your specialty, get back in the kitchen.

Ultimately, what you need is to take a risk and do something to bring yourself back to life. I'm not advocating this is the first six months, or even the first eight months (although, if you're ready, you should go for it). But, after nine or 10 months, you may start to feel an itch. You want to return to *yourself,* the self who wasn't afraid to live because you might make a mistake and end up like your husband (meaning: you'll die).

Releasing this fear that you'll die if you make a mistake, choose the wrong path, or err in your judgment, is the real beginning of confidence. Confidence, ultimately, will lead to your complete healing.

Guidelines for Gaining Confidence

1. Practice self-awareness to determine which of your activities builds self-esteem.

2. Make room in your life for this special activity.

3. If you feel excitement over a project or plan—the confidence gained just by *trying* it is worth it.

4. Let yourself indulge in former activities you know made you feel empowered: planting roses in your garden; helping children learn to read; organizing a fund-raiser at your church, even tackling a super hard project at work that nobody else wants to do. You know how those special efforts galvanized your energies and made you stand tall. Now is the time to indulge in this again.

5. Consciously pat yourself on the back for your efforts. You're doing great!

Chapter Thirty-Three

Aging

I've mentioned the common occurrence after losing your husband, of assuming that you, too, will soon die. This conviction doesn't happen to everyone, and it's not an ongoing or even lasting condition of widowhood, but if you're getting up there in years (or even if you're not; a 50-year old widow told me she'd experienced the state), chances are you will succumb to premonitions of death at least once in your first year of widowhood.

And why not? Everyone dies, and it is only culture's rather silly stigma against talking about it openly that causes the fear, or shall we say, *panic.*

I'm not talking about the practical steps some widows take soon after their husband's death to ensure that they too will have a nice memorial service, or a pleasant place to lie beside their loved one. While this may be related, what I'm referring to is the nameless fear that your own death is imminent.

You can relax. This feeling is entirely normal; in fact, most of the widows I've talked to have reported experiencing it at least once. The state can have any number of forms: a superstitious conviction that you will join hubby on the anniversary of the first month of his passing, or an almost compulsive urge to guard against dust, food preservatives, traffic noise, and anything that might bring on some deadly virus that will ultimately do you in.

If you haven't experienced any of these states, you might, instead, find yourself plagued by a weird feeling of unreality—as if the space you now inhabit is not your real life. "If I turn around," you think, "I'll find myself back in my comfort zone—with him."

All these symptoms are part of grieving, and you don't need to feel there's something particularly wrong with you for feeling them (unless they never go away—in which case you might want to consult a friendly therapist). Feelings of unreality, and a preoccupation with your own death—yes, that's grieving, girl.

However, there is something you can do to ease this particular pain. It has to do with aging.

We live in a country obsessed with youth and the goings-on of young people. If you think this obsession is just particular to our times, think again. Remember the mania over hula-hoops? Beehive hairdos? The Beatles? It seems every generation focuses on youth's predilections, and why not? We love our children, want to see them happy, and yes—we do identify with them.

What does this have to do with aging? Quite simply, as long as we are vicariously following the fancies of young people, we are, in our minds, "still young." I'm not suggesting that we all go out and get ourselves pierced here, there, and everywhere, or spend our entire lives looking at Facebook. But—stay abreast, as soon as you are able. You can join Facebook; it won't hurt you. Buy a fashion magazine and note the new styles; see if you can go out and purchase one item that is this year's fashion. Find a trendy perfume. (Do you know a 20-year old? Ask her which one to buy.) Adopt your "signature" scent. Take a walk around the block, and feel the wind in your face as you move your legs; it's remarkable how much a simple walk can do to offset that disconcerting sense of "I'm getting old!"

Remember, your husband died—you didn't. Not yet. You may have many years of living to do, or you may have just a few. As a widow, you have probably experienced something valuable to you and others—you have experienced wisdom. Now do ahead, dear widow—use it.

Guidelines for Aging

1. Buy the newest cell phone you can afford, the one with the most apps—and learn how to use it.

2. Go see one of the "Twilight Saga" movies (or whatever film is currently being embraced by young people).

3. Watch "Sex and the City" reruns (this has nothing to do with sex—yes, I know you're not ready, but the ongoing dissection of relationships can be very stimulating.)

4. Look at what's trending on the Internet.

5. Find a popular perfume or fragrance and adopt is as your own. Perfume is something you can wear without worrying about whether or not it's "too young" for you.

6. Read a fashion magazine and go shopping for yourself.

7. Start exercising some way as soon as you are able—a walk around the block is a great way to start. Part of the ill effects of mourning are from the way that you are living in your head. Get re-acquainted with your body.

8. Take a little weekend trip away, by yourself. Define what "widow" means to you.

9. Keep a journal of your progress with "aging" beautifully.

10. Celebrate your birthday, and not necessarily with a party. (Depending upon when your birthday falls, you may feel it's inappropriate to celebrate with a party.)

a. Go away by yourself to a spa or some nice hotel with room service.

b. Be a kid again, and visit a theme part or other famous attraction—often such places are free to local residents on their birthdays.

c. Indulge yourself in a day of pampering, including lunching out, shopping, a massage or new haircut, a movie or a museum visit.

d. Acknowledge your love for your dearly departed, and remember, he'd want you to be happy on your birthday.

11. Do something you used to enjoy ten years ago. (For me, this meant going to the beach. Totally enjoyable— and youth enhancing, even though I now use Sun Block #45 instead of baby oil.)

12. Set a little challenge for yourself—attend a conference, drive non-stop to see an old friend, or submit a painting to the next "Art Walk." Take a risk, however small. Surviving that risk can give you a new lease on life.

Chapter Thirty-Four

Cleaning Out Hubby's Closet

At the time of this writing—two weeks before Thanksgiving—I have not yet finished cleaning out my husband's closet. I've been a widow for ten months, but I don't feel bad about my procrastination, and neither should you.

I started this task early on, or fairly early in my estimation. About 12 weeks into my widowhood I began selecting some of my husband's good clothes and donating them to AmVets, an organization that helps veterans and their families. Since Jack was a veteran, I felt this was the right thing to do. My donations went on for about a month, every week. Since this was also the period of time when I was visiting the VA in an effort to discover if Jack had ever stepped foot in Vietnam, perhaps there was a connection.

When I had gone through most of the good clothes, I began cleaning out dresser drawers. Most of this went to the Salvation Army containers on street corners, and here is where it began to hurt. I remember dumping a bag of socks, T-shirts and shorts into the receptacle and thinking, "I can't do this anymore."

I didn't analyze why I couldn't do it, or beat myself up for not being able to do it. I just remember that I closed the door on that activity for an unspecified amount of time.

That was early May, about six months ago. I haven't touched Jack's closet since. I can't; it's still too painful. Also, I feel I need a sort of "buffer zone" of time to finish the task, which I've not had in the last few months (first there was the editing of my friend Karen's book, then returning full time to the academic world in August).

Who am I kidding? If I'd wanted to clean out the closet, and if I'd been capable of doing it, there was time. I had time to go shopping on the weekends; I had time to go to Seashore National Park and write; I had plenty of time for lunches and dinners with my girlfriends these last 10 months, but the closet—no, there was no time for that. Cleaning out the closet needed "special time," time to prepare myself before, and comfort myself after.

Have you found yourself in this situation? There always seems to be more important things to do than clean out the closet, or conversely, cleaning out the closet is of such monumental importance that it needs its own special day, or week, or month to accomplish, and we're not ready to give it that time—yet.

The real reason, of course, is that we don't want to say goodbye. There is something about cleaning out the closet that signals the end like no other task. So we wait, and hesitate, and procrastinate, hoping for the perfect moment to touch us like a wand.

What if the perfect moment never comes? Sure, we've all heard of widows and widowers who never finished cleaning out the closet, who go on two years, three years, five, even ten years with hubby's clothes still hanging on hangers, waiting to be sorted out and given away. Someone suggested giving shirts to a relative, but this I couldn't do. I couldn't bear to see Jack's shirt on a cousin or nephew—ouch! (It was hard enough recently noting that a colleague at my college was wearing the same shirt that I'd given Jack one Christmas, but I didn't know the man, and didn't see him or the shirt again.)

Maybe you've had this experience of seeing your husband's clothes on someone else. A sweater, or a jacket you glimpsed from the back. Oh my, it's him, you think, but you know it isn't—by now you know it isn't. Yet the little twinge gets to you; you wonder what it's all about, this process of grieving. Shouldn't you be over it by now?

Although the pain of grieving is supposed to subside within a year, according to Hospice, the process of grieving may go on much longer. We may not be ready to say "good-bye" in a year, or two or three. Does it matter? Is it anyone's business but ours? I don't think so.

Cleaning out the closet may be a way for us to measure how far along we are in the grieving process. If that's the case, I'm not done yet.

Guidelines for Cleaning Out the Closet

1. This is your affair, and no one else's. Do not be influenced by timetables dictating when and how this process should occur.

2. Realize that even though you may be holding down a full-time job, managing a household, even enjoying a social life, "the closet" can still be a formidable task. That's because it entails your emotions, and emotions heal slowly.

3. Don't force yourself to do it before you're ready.

4. Find a charity you like and donate some of the good clothes—it helps to imagine a needy individual being aided by your gift.

5. Be gentle with yourself, dear widow. This is one of the hardest tasks for most of us. It's not like clearing out your deceased parents' closets; it's more like cleaning out your own. Don't do it until you can do it easily.

Chapter Thirty-Five

Photographs

There is nothing so poignant as a photograph of someone who is no longer with you. If that someone is your husband, the picture is doubly moving, because you are face to face with an image that still resonates in your mind with a multitude of accompanying emotions. You see the face, but inside your mind you have a different image—alive, smiling, frowning, talking, laughing—the ongoing memory of that man you know so well.

Photographs can be a vital part of your healing, because they provide a link from the past, which is in the photo, to whatever way you are going to think about your husband in the future. As I've mentioned, I have a laminated bookmark with Jack's picture that I keep in the front of my journal. Every morning as I prepare to write in the journal, I pick up the bookmark and look at Jack's photo. Sometimes I kiss it. Sometimes I ask a question and get an answer that is typical of something Jack might have said—witty, loving, and a tiny bit inclined to give advice. No, I'm not talking to my dead spouse—I'm imagining a comment based on my best recollection of my husband. Jack had a terrific sense of humor; the photograph on the bookmark, a smiling image, brings back this wonderful humor to me every day, because Jack, a man I knew for 43 years, is so much a part of me that he and his personality will never go away.

I have other photographs of my husband around the house, and, of course, pictures of the two of us. There is a wedding photo from 1969, where we both look younger than the students I'm teaching now (we weren't). There is a little photo of us from 1974, taken at the house in Woodstock we shared with other people (not a commune; that was earlier). In this photo, Jack had mid-length hair and had shaved off his mustache, and I'm wearing a blue jean jacket and a "Jane Fonda haircut."

There is a photo from 1991 of the two of us with the artist Edna Hibbel, Jack holding a video camera, and me looking efficient in a black jumpsuit. That picture surfaced after Jack's death, which is the reason I have it on display. And then there are the most recent photos, from the last year of his life—a photo of Jack that I took standing on a deck by the beach, his hair ruffled, and a smile on his face. I love that picture.

Jack was a motion picture photographer in the Army in 1963, and after that, he made his living shooting and editing film, video and still photos. There are boxes and boxes of photographs in my house, as there probably are in yours. I am not spending much time going through them right now, but I will. Like you, I'm awfully glad those photos are around. If I want to see how my husband looked at age 28, 40, 55, 63, or 70—all I have to do is look at a photograph, and I will remember…everything.

Guidelines for Photographs

1. Select one favorite photo of your husband, and place it where you will see it every day. This will provide an amazing amount of comfort to you.

2. Don't hide, or put away, or change any of the photos of your husband that you have displayed in your house—no matter how blue you may be feeling on any

particular day. Remember, time will heal your heart, and you'll want those photos around when you're feeling yourself again.

3. Use your photographs as a way to communicate your feelings about your husband. Even if this brings tears, photos of your husband can facilitate your healing.

4. Don't turn away from a photo of your husband, even if it brings you pain. Pain is love in this circumstance. The more you can embrace your pain, the more your love will deepen. Ultimately, the pain will diffuse into a bittersweet memory, which becomes sweeter as time goes by.

5. Look at your photographs as a pathway to your own growth. Love continues beyond death, and love brings wisdom, patience, and growth.

Chapter Thirty-Six

Survivor Guilt

Just when you think you're over the worst of your grieving, it jumps back and takes a swipe at you. And because you've relaxed your guard a little, this go-round is especially painful.

I had been on the job about two and a half months when I began to notice little signs that something was amiss in my emotional well-being. First of all, I was waking up at 2 or 3 a.m., after just a few hours sleep, and worrying about things at my job, little things, like whether the nametags would be finished on time, or whether the Conference program would turn out okay. (Teaching public relations, I was in charge of two events—one of them a class project.)

Then, after an hour or two of worrying about inconsequential things, I'd begin to think about Jack. I'd wonder if I'd done anything wrong in my care for him that last year—I'd speculate on whether he'd still be alive "if only I'd..." and so on. It was useless and painful speculation.

The other red flag sign was that I'd started putting on weight. Instead of leaving one-third on my plate (okay, usually I left one-fourth on my plate, but it still worked)—I'd gobble up the whole thing and go back for seconds. Now, this is okay once in a while, but if it becomes an everyday habit, weight gain is usually the result. Soon, my pants were getting too tight, and my self-esteem was dropping.

Then, one night, after about three weeks of my semi-insomnia, I woke up in a panic. There was a buzzing in my ears that I couldn't seem to control. What was it? Anxiety? About what? My responsibilities at work? Or—Jack? I tried writing in my journal, and found it hard. Finally, I had to turn everything over to God, and this is what I wrote:

"It's guilt—survivor guilt. I'm here and Jack isn't. I am here, thinking about life and things to do, and Jack isn't here, doing any of this. I feel guilty about Jack. No matter what I think I've done, what I accuse myself of, the truth is that I feel guilty I'm still alive.

"But I'm not God. Only God takes life and gives life—I don't. That's the truth. If I believe in God, I must believe this.

"Am I in a depression? Maybe. If I am, then I know how to handle it—exactly what I've been doing since Day One of Jack's passing, only more so. God is stronger than depression.

"To have faith in God is to lose the fear of death. So maybe what I have is a fear of depression. I'm doing so well! I have all these blessings! Let me make a list."

Then I wrote a list of blessings, such as the one given in the Appendix of this book—and got back to sleep for another hour or two.

This went on for about a week—waking in the middle of the night and "battling" with myself. I began talking it over with friends, a very good thing to do. At our age, almost everyone has lost a family member or two, or three or four. Everyone has ways to cope.

I began to realize, with the help of my boss (a friend), that my perfectionism on the job was hurting me. It was a source of anxiety, which triggered other anxieties. If you go through anything like this, you may find other causes—friction with adults or children, or a new health ailment for instance. These are triggers for the real source of your anxiety: the fact that you are still alive, and your husband isn't.

So what can you do? Lots. You can see a therapist, and I seriously considered it at this point. You can deal with the "trigger"—in my case, perfectionism on the job, and try to alleviate that. You can also go back to your extreme nurturing (see Chapter Three). You're hurting, and when you're hurting you need love.

So I started going out to lunch rather than eating a salad in my office at school. I bought some new outfits, saw some movies, and went out to dinner with my girlfriends during the week, not just on weekends. In other words, I paid attention to my pain—and took care of myself.

After a while, the buzzing in my ears stopped. I quit beating up on myself and cut back on some of my work responsibilities. I accepted the fact that, yes, I was still alive, had a life to live, and my husband was no longer here. That's the reality of things.

In most obituaries, Jack's included, the final section is devoted to the family members who are still alive. In Jack's obituary it reads: "Mr. Milton is survived by his wife, Joanna; two sisters..." etc. *Survived by*, meaning, we are still alive. That's just the way it is, and there's nothing to feel guilty about.

Guidelines for Dealing with Survivor Guilt

1. If you find yourself going through some unexplained behavioral changes—insomnia, loss of appetite or over-eating—pay attention! Something is going on, and you may need to see a therapist.

2. Step up the self-nurturing, and cut back on any anxiety-producing activities at work or at home.

3. Write about what you're going through—it may point the way toward a salvation.

4. Talk with friends, and explain what's going on—don't hide your feelings.

5. Realize you are still in mourning, even if you don't want to be. Even if you're holding down a full-time job, and doing it well, chairing a volunteer organization, dealing with sick relatives or doing other time-consuming activities—you are still grieving the loss of your husband. Don't cut it short.

Part Four: Learning to be You

Chapter Thirty-Seven

Wedding Ring

My friend Liz, now widowed six years, told me that it was not until she moved her wedding ring from her left hand to her right that she knew for sure she was healed. I myself have not made that transition. Mine still sits comfortably on my left hand's third finger, a reminder that so very recently, I had a husband. It's a comfort, a remembrance, and a security blanket. *No, I'm not alone; I still have the fresh memory of my husband—see, here's his ring.*

Liz also told me that when she changed hands for her ring, she knew she was ready to meet other men. (She did not tell me when that transition happened, and I didn't ask; the wedding ring, like cleaning the closet, is one of those very personal aspects that is nobody's business but your own. If you're interested, I will tell you that, as of right now, I have no plans of removing my ring just yet.)

My wedding ring is a simple gold band that Jack and I purchased together in Key West two days before we got married the second time. My "engagement" ring is a blue Topaz in the shape of a heart that he bought for me when we got back together in 1990. Our first set of rings were long gone—a handmade combo, involving gold and rubies, purchased in the Village at an artsy-hippie jewelers in 1969. We hippies didn't cotton to show; just getting married was "establishment" enough.

I suppose one of these days I will remove my wedding ring and decide to make myself available to other men—or maybe not. Perhaps I am waiting for one of my friends to say, "Ye Gods, are you still wearing your wedding ring?" If it's two, or three, or five years after my husband's passing, I'll probably pay attention to that remark, but right now—no. (And fortunately, no one has said it.)

How much love is one allowed in one lifetime? I've been married three times, although twice to the same man. All three marriages were consecrated in love, and love alone. Not money, not position, not "because it's the right thing to do," or "it's time." Do I have any right to expect that love will enter my life another time? Do I even want it to?

My friend Liz told me that after a couple of years she decided she liked things as they were; she liked being independent. I have an idea I may be the same (although a love affair would probably be okay).

If that's the case—if I choose to remain single—then perhaps it's all right to wear Jack's ring as long as I feel comfortable doing so. It's a sign, a symbol that I committed myself to a man—how brave!

As I said, it's nobody's business but my own.

Guidelines for the Wedding Ring

Just one—It is your decision, and yours alone, to remove your wedding ring. Wear it as long as you want.

Chapter Thirty-Eight

How to Tell When You're Getting Better

You're getting better when it no longer hurts to cry. Your tears are tinged with gratitude; you feel blessed that you've had all the good times you enjoyed with your husband.

You're getting better when you look in the mirror and like the face you see. It's no longer somehow foreign to you, or sad, or plain, or just a blank. All of a sudden, you see a little of your old spark, your old beauty. Yes, you were beautiful once, weren't you! Back when you and he were young, playing with love, and wrapped up in each other. We were all beautiful once, and suddenly, you see a glimpse of that girl again—it's "something in the way she moves," as the old Beatles song goes.

You're getting better when you start thinking about sex again. I don't mean sexual fantasies—those can happen very early on, and they're not really a sign of anything, except that you're normal. I'm talking about thinking of actually doing it, not imagining it graphically, but practically: What about those five pounds I've put on since hubby died? Should I invite (whomever it is) to dinner first? That way we're already in the vicinity of the bedroom...

You may or may not have someone in mind for this assignment. It almost doesn't matter; the mere fact that you're even thinking about such a move means—you're on the mend.

You're getting better when you start contemplating what you want to do the next year, and the next. You realize you haven't died—maybe it's time for a new list. Something may have occurred to stimulate this reaction: perhaps a new project has opened up that you really want to tackle. Maybe you're been offered a promotion or a new job, or maybe there was some other event that made you stop and think about the future. (Yes, you have a future.) Maybe some freak occurrence has jolted you into the present (like my experience with Pandora)—and you say, "Hey, I want to know what's going to happen *tomorrow*..."

Whatever the reason, these triggers are there to alert you to the fact that things have changed since the early days of your mourning. You do not love your husband less, or miss him any less poignantly, but he is no longer with you every step of the way. You realize that he has traveled on to wherever one goes, and you cannot go there. You have your own path to follow. Your husband does not want to hold you back now, just as he did not hold you back in life. If you are reluctant to let go, okay, that's normal, but if a part of you is starting to get just a little curious about what is going to happen next—dear widow, you are definitely coming out of the shadows.

Guidelines for Telling When You are Getting Better

1. Instead of feeling weepy when you look at his picture, you crack a one-liner, like "Hey, how am I doing?" (Remember New York Mayor Ed Koch?)

2. You go out and buy something out of the ordinary to wear, because it makes you feel sexy, or cuddly, or a little bit different. Even if you don't wear it right away, you know it's in your closet.

3. You can have dinner with a girlfriend and not mention your husband except in passing.

4. You can watch a romantic movie and enjoy it without feeling lonesome for your husband. (You may, however, feel a pleasant sense of camaraderie, such as..."we were like that once.")

5. You start looking at other men. (Now, if this doesn't happen, don't worry. Not all women, or even most, want to get involved with anyone this soon, but you might just become aware of other men as *men*, and that's okay.)

Spontaneity and Changing Your Mind

It has been said that it's a woman's right to change her mind. As a new widow, you have double that right, because not only are you a woman, you're a woman who has been through a *lot*. Your emotions have pulled you in this direction and that, after spinning you around and placing you back in a place you think you should have left long ago. You've made advances, and gone weeks without shedding a tear, only to find yourself breaking down over a TV commercial advertising socks, or cereal, or the charms of vacationing in California. (Oh! You and hubby had talked about a trip out West and now it will never happen...)

So, yes, you can change your mind—change it as often as you like. The first year of widowhood is a time of transition: you know who you *were*—a wife, maybe a caretaker, and part of a couple, to be sure—but you don't exactly know who you're going to be when you've adjusted completely to the state of being a widow.

Are you going to be a working woman again, devoting yourself to your job as you've never been able to do before because of family obligations? Are you going to be a creative, contemplative woman, dreaming away the hours as you indulge yourself in hobbies that have always been pushed aside—your painting, your pottery, your jewelry making, or your gardening? Or are you going to become a modern Auntie Mame, traveling the world without a care as you live, live, live! Maybe a little of all three?

It would be easy to say, "I'll wait to decide until a clear direction emerges," but usually it doesn't work that way. Usually we try a little of this, a little of that, take a bite of this direction, reject it, and go for another—in other words, we *change our minds.*

My own situation is a case in point. After accepting a full-time faculty position when I'd initially agreed to just part-time teaching, I found half-way through that perhaps I should have gone with my first instinct. In the early days of the semester I'd envisioned myself the dedicated teacher, now staying late and working on weekends at the college, as I'd never been able to do before. But in fact, I didn't *want* to work late and on weekends—I wanted to go out to dinner with my friends after work; I wanted to write at the beach on the weekends. These options were much more appealing to me than going into an empty school building and pounding away on a computer. So the dedicated teacher idea sort of fizzled, and in fact, as the semester became more stressful, I began to wish I had stuck to my original part-time plan. I decided to bow out of the situation, telling my supervisor I'd only be available for part-time work the following semester.

Yet I didn't consider taking on the full-time position as a "mistake"—I'd proved to myself I could do it, and do it well. The fact that my emotions weren't completely healed was just a sign that I needed more time for healing. Hospice says it takes at least a year to go through the grieving process, and I'd only given it ten months.

While I am on the subject of changing one's mind, let me add a word about spontaneity. Although I am an advocator of lists, we cannot be too locked into our plans (especially if they are on the austere side.) As we begin to heal, it's a good idea to be open to new ideas—focusing in particular on those ideas that bring us comfort and joy in any form.

I have two good friends who are widows, Anne and Marie. Both of them have taught me how to encourage spontaneity and flexibility, even in midst grieving and healing. Anne's husband passed on suddenly at the age of 62. After a suitable amount of time had passed—about a year—Anne sold her house in the suburbs of New York and moved closer to the city, where she worked. She also started a part-time business in addition to her full-time job. Then a while later, she quite the full-time job and began to develop her part-time business into a full-time profession. This is what is meant by "reinventing" one's self, and of course, you don't have to be a widow to do it—but many widows do. Since Anne's new business is not dependent on location, she is now planning to move to another state, "one with a little less winter than New York," she told me.

Marie's life is equally as spontaneous. Bereaved of her beloved husband in her 40s, she married again, combining two large families. When her second husband died, she moved to another city, went back to school and began a new career in her 60s. She is now a healer and teacher. She is an inspiring woman, who has taken pain and upheaval and turned it into channels for helping others.

Spontaneity does not necessarily have to involve huge life choices; in fact, as stated often in this book, it's probably better not to make major decisions the first year of widowhood, but you can practice your spontaneity in small ways. For instance, the Saturday after Thanksgiving I'd planned a full day of work—grading papers, housecleaning, and moving boxes out of Jack's business building. I'd noticed a twinge of sadness when I woke in the morning—I'd survived Thanksgiving with hardly a tear (well, a few tears, but what can you expect?) I'd celebrated the holiday at a friend's house, socialized again on Friday, and had plans for Sunday—yet my Saturday "catch-up" day no longer seemed appealing. As I began my chores, I felt my heart sinking—what was wrong? I wasn't socially deprived...

But here's the thing: as a new widow, your feelings, as you've probably found out, do not always follow a logical path. So, even if you've been doing fine following your lists, and you think you're making progress healing, don't be surprised if, unexpectedly, you find yourself wanting to break out of your routine.

I'm not saying we should quit our jobs on a moment's notice, or pack off to Hawaii if we don't have the funds to support such a trip, but a little spontaneity may be just what is needed. That particular day I rescheduled my paper grading—the only task I really had to do—and took off for Coldwater Creek, where I had a couple of nice coupons. I bought Christmas presents, and a lovely sweater for myself, and then went to Panera for a peppermint mocha and a cherry pastry. Needless to say, the blues disappeared, and I was able to catch up on housecleaning and moving boxes the following week.

Being flexible and being spontaneous is like opening a big present to yourself. It is the gift of *you*, and it's a gift you need to give yourself—again, and again, and again.

(By the way...at this point, I'm planning to teach just two courses in the spring, but who knows; I could change my mind again...)

Guidelines for Spontaneity and Changing Your Mind

1. Be aware of subtle (and not so subtle) fluctuations in your feelings and give them respect. Remember, you are evolving constantly. What may have seemed like a good idea in the third month of widowhood may no longer suit you in the tenth.

2. While we don't necessarily want to make major life changes during the first year of widowhood, we do want to consider them. Give the spontaneous suggestion that comes to you in the middle of the night or while you are taking a drive just as much attention as anything you've put on one of your lists.

3. Practice little acts of spontaneity before you spread your wings for a major change. Put your running shoes on and go for a jog around the block, even though it's almost dark and a bit on the chilly side. The idea came to you, and you're up for it. Schedule a little vacation for yourself during the holidays; sign up for that course in "Learning Spanish" at the community college. Try a new hair color, go bowling, or redecorate your bedroom. These are not major life changes—yet they may give you a new lease on life.

4. Don't let yourself be forced into any kind of widow-mold. If you don't want to spend every Sunday with the family, don't do so. Don't stay in a stifling job, don't bottle up your sensuality, and don't dress in drab colors just because you think it's expected of you. In reality, a lot of these "should do" and "should not do" stigmas are in our own minds. Our family and friends want what is best for us, and only we know what that is.

5. Change your mind about anything and everything as often as you like, until you come up with the "you" that you're meant to be.

Chapter Forty

Dating

There's no correct time to begin dating after your husband dies, and in fact, if you'd prefer not to—that's okay too. I know a couple of widows who got married seven or eight months after bereavement—others shut the door on the whole intimate relationship thing and felt just fine about it.

I ventured out dancing about eleven months after Jack's passing. A friend had suggested it—not a buddy-type friend, but someone I'd known for several years. I was pretty reluctant about the idea of dating, and had turned down a couple of fix-ups, but a week earlier I'd seen the remake of "Footloose" and felt inspired to hit the dance floor. I'd always loved to dance, and Jack and I had continued dancing regularly (I'm not talking ballroom dancing, I mean the real stuff, where you end up sweating if you're doing it right)—well into our 60s.

When we first moved to Daytona Beach, Jack and I went to a place called the Ocean Deck and danced to Caribbean Posse, a reggae band that also played an assortment of rock music. On my first "date" with Alan, we went to the Ocean Deck too, only it was quite a bit different. Not *bad*, just different. In most respects, it was pretty good.

Alan and I had arranged to meet at the Ocean Deck at 9 p.m., about the time the band came on. I arrived on time, glided into the lounge and took a seat at the bar. It was off-season and not too crowded. (There are times at the Ocean

Deck when one can barely move through the throngs of people.) I ordered a glass of Chardonnay and sat there sipping it, congratulating myself on not feeling the least uncomfortable about sitting at a bar, alone on a Friday night. Of course, I had my wedding ring on. I'd decided not to remove it for my date—I wasn't interested in anything romantic with Alan. I just wanted to dance.

Twenty minutes later, I was still sipping, and starting to feel a little bit irked. What, was I going to be stood up on my very first date? It hardly seemed possible—Alan had asked me out twice before I'd agreed. Two stools down at the bar, a guy about my age ventured to make an innocuous comment about the band: I pretended I didn't hear him. I did not come here to be picked up, for God's sake. I glanced at my watch, deciding to leave at 9:45—ten minutes to go.

I was already thinking about a cozy evening of TV in my pajamas and eating some chocolate cake, when I saw Alan coming out of the men's room. He glanced toward me and I waved; "You're late," I said sternly, when he approached.

"What do you mean, I've been here 45 minutes—over there, at that table." He pointed toward the back room—well, of course he'd sit at a table, I thought, not at the bar where you can hardly hear a thing when the band starts.

But that's where Jack always liked to sit—at the bar. So instinctively, that's where I'd chosen to plant myself.

Things got better after that—we danced, and talked, and danced some more. Once out on the dance floor, I noticed that the drummer was the same guy who'd been in the band when Jack and I first started going to the Ocean Deck. "Look," I said, motioning to Alan—"That guy has been here for 20 years!" The significance may have been lost on Alan, because he didn't seem particularly interested in this information. But I was impressed—20 years of drumming at the

Ocean Deck, and maybe a third of those who'd heard him 20 years ago were no longer alive.

During the evening I mentioned "Jack" and "my husband" several times, and Alan didn't seem to mind. He knew all about it because, after all, we were friends. It seemed natural to me to refer to my husband because, frankly, I felt Jack was there too that night.

I didn't really want to go home, but at 12:30 I felt I had to, since I had movers coming the next day. Since we'd arrived in two cars (definitely a good idea), and I'd valet parked (an even better idea), there was no awkward goodbye, but I don't think there would have been anyway—Alan was too much of a gentleman, and we hadn't really worked up a sweat...

No, it wasn't like the old days with Jack. How could it be? I was still in love with my husband and always would be, but I do like to dance!

Guidelines for Dating

1. Wait until you're absolutely ready before going out with anyone—and if you never feel ready, so be it. There's no rule stating you must date.

2. For your first post-bereavement experience, go out with a friend. It's going to be hard enough doing what you're doing without the onus of trying to get to know a stranger.

3. Take separate cars. You're used to traveling around alone by now; this is just one more experience where you are calling the shots.

4. If there's valet parking—use it. (You may even opt for a place with valet parking because it takes the worry out of leaving.)

5. Don't expect too much. You're probably going to think of your husband during the evening—maybe more than once. It's not going to be like a first date in your

teens, or 20s, or even 40s. You're a widow (and it's okay to wear your wedding ring).

Chapter Forty-One

Exercise

I admit it: I haven't gotten as much exercise as I should have these last few months. In fact, my main form of exercise seems to be running up and down the stairs of the Fine Arts building at the college where I teach. I say "run," but it's more like a slow walk, balancing books, papers, notebooks and, of course, my five-pound handbag.

Lately I've been dancing on Friday nights with my friend Alan. A couple of hours of vigorous exercise can slim you down a bit (at least, I'm hoping it will). During winter and spring I was frequenting the swimming pool at the Y and swimming laps until the kids got out of school. Then it became difficult to get a lap in because of their summer camp schedule, which seemed to encompass almost all of the daylight hours from 10-6. So I repaired to the beach, managing a 20 minute walk two or three times a week.

Not enough, really, but as a new widow, you may find if difficult to squeeze in time for something as non-essential as exercise in the midst of all the organizing of your husband's affairs and your own attempts to regain sanity.

Hey! Wait a minute—did I just say non-essential? Big mistake. Let's face it: exercise, at this particular time, is more than just keeping yourself "fit" in the standard, lets-be-healthy way. Exercise is a form of self-care and anything remotely connected with self-care must be given a high priority on your Things To Do list.

Exercise is a way for you to connect with and increase awareness of yourself in your body, an awareness that you may not always be feeling these days. During the stress of early widowhood, your consciousness may be all over the place: Sometimes you can feel your heart beating loudly in your ears; at other times, your mind seems to be on a loop of obsessive thoughts so persistent that you don't even know who you are anymore. This is part of grief, and, unfortunately, the physical component of grief can seem to negate the normal self-awareness we have of our bodies. The result is a sort of "out of body" experience that is most disconcerting, if not downright unpleasant.

Exercise is a way for us to put ourselves back into our bodies, to "ground" our thought into an awareness of limbs, muscles, arms, legs, feet and hands. For someone who has been flying around in her head and worrying for hours on end, this grounding can feel like sublime pleasure. Suddenly, we are "there"; we feel our arms reaching out to cut the water in a breast stroke, we see our calves as we relax after our swim, and we admire the muscle tone, the smooth skin, and the flex of a foot. In short, during and after exercise, we are out of our heads for a restful interlude while we bask in the simplicity and beauty of our bodies.

I say beauty on purpose, because even if we don't always like the way we look, there is something about exercise that makes us appreciate our physical form. Call it norepinephrine or keeping up with the Jones's, but the high that most of us get after exercising is worth any discomfort that may occur in the process. Exercise is love; it is a form of self-love that, for the widow, can provide a unique link to healing. Through exercise we move, we breathe, and we realize that we are still in the world. That, dear widow, is a large part of our goal: to celebrate the fact that we are alive.

Guidelines for Exercise

1. If you look at exercise as a pathway to healing, rather than as a fitness routine, you may find yourself more interested in participating.

2. Begin an exercise regime slowly, allowing yourself to enjoy the feeling of your legs walking, your arms stretching, and the twist of your torso.

3. Learn to appreciate each tiny change in your body as your health and suppleness improve. Appreciating your body is part of finding a balance between your mind and the outer world—a balance you are constantly trying to re-establish during widowhood.

4. Don't push yourself while exercising—allow the activity to surround you, and lift you up.

5. Be grateful that you are exercising!

Chapter Forty-Two

His Birthday

In the 1989 movie, "Chances Are," Cybill Shepherd celebrates the birthday of her husband by making him his favorite dish. Later, going to bed, she offers his photo a chocolate before turning out the light. This might not seem too unusual except for the fact that Cybill's husband has been dead 23 years.

Of course, it's only a movie. We all have different ways of commemorating birthdays, our husband's and our own. While our methods may not be as drastic as Cybill Shepherd's character in "Chances Are," what we choose to do in the privacy of our own personal lives may range from the sublime to the peculiar, depending on our frame of mind. And our frame of mind is going to be influenced by how far along we are in our widowhood when that birthday shows up.

My husband's birthday came almost at the end of my first year of widowhood. I was well on the way to recovery, so I didn't think the occasion would grieve me. I wished Jack a happy birthday and gave his bookmark photograph a kiss. I wrote in my journal about the day but did not shed any tears doing so (which I would have done if the day had come two or even one month earlier). No, I thought, I'm okay—so I proceeded to get ready for a Christmas party I'd been invited to and didn't give the birthday much more thought.

At the party I told two very close friends, Karen and Marie, that the day marked Jack's birthday. Both of them looked at me sympathetically and murmured comforting words. Before I could get emotional, however, Karen said to Marie, "Isn't Joanna doing well!" Marie agreed and a flush of pleasure suffused me, knocking out my sadness. "Thank you," I murmured, grateful for the rescue.

Both friends were very attentive to me that day, as they had been all year, and I had a lovely time at the party. But later, driving home, waves of memory pulsed through me—Jack would have been 72, still so young it seemed, in the greater scheme of things. Unwilling to go home, I stopped by a Starbucks and bought a Café Mocha and a brownie (Jack loved brownies, although I've never been wild about them myself), and then I drove out to the Seashore National Park. It was nearing sunset, and the light over the water was pure and sweet.

There, in that safe harbor, I shed a few tears—just a few because so much had happened during the year. Since losing Jack, I had grieved, made a plan, and grieved some more. I had learned how to be alone, sometimes willingly, other times not so willingly. I had gone shopping more this past year than any year since my dad's death, because shopping helped me. I had lunched with friends and alone, engaged in a writing project, and helped others with their plans. I had cleaned out part of my husband's closet, taken on a full-time job, gone through some major holidays, and I'd prayed—oh boy, had I prayed.

And while I am grateful that my friends think I'm doing well, I myself know there is still some healing to be done. Regardless of what Hospice may say, I don't believe one year is enough to get over the loss of one's husband.

And so on this, my husband's birthday, I write with tears in my eyes, thinking of Cybill Shepherd's character in

"Chances Are," and her gift of chocolate to her dead husband's photo. No, I'm not going to offer Jack a bite of brownie, but I think it's significant that I bought one, don't you?

Guidelines for His Birthday

1. By all means, recognize the fact that it is your late husband's birthday and you miss him.

2. Try to plan some diversion so that you won't be sitting home alone. This is a holiday of sorts, and needs to be treated with the same caution and respect that other holidays receive during your early widowhood—even though you are the only one involved.

3. Allow friends to comfort you by telling them what day it is.

4. Cry, and realize that you might shed a few tears every year on this date. Or you might not.

5. Try not to overdo it in any one direction. Rituals have a habit of becoming permanent, and you probably don't want to prepare an elaborate dinner for your dearly departed since you might feel obligated to do the same thing the following year. Leave that for the movies.

Chapter Forty-Three

Other Women's Husbands

Do some widows re-marry just so they can maintain relationships with their married women friends? It would seem so, since being around other women's husbands, if you're a widow, is like walking through a minefield. You step gingerly, because, if you're reasonably attractive, it seems your friends' husbands will go out of their way to try to please you. Of course, they're just trying to be nice, and I appreciate that—but their wives (your girlfriends) don't always realize these innocent motives.

I have heard stories of widows being ostracized from social gatherings in communities where they once held places of high regard. I do not live in a suburb, where such behavior seems to happen, but I do have one personal example of the case in point. Several years ago I was in a situation where a close friend of my husband died, leaving a lonely widow whom Jack had known for over 30 years. So it seemed natural that he should comfort Annette, bringing her flowers when we went to dinner at her house, and calling her on the phone to wish her happy birthday.

I wasn't thrilled about it—and when Annette gave Jack her spouse's car, I became a little worried. Was she becoming infatuated with my husband? He swore there was nothing going on, and in time, his actions proved this was true, but I learned something about widowhood during this experience. Annette told Jack that all her married friends had stopped inviting her to their homes soon after her husband died. This seems like a particularly cruel thing for a widow to endure, and if you don't want this to happen to you, you must bend over backward to avoid anything that even looks like flirting with your friends' husbands. Remember, they're just trying to be nice—and even if they're doing more than being nice, it is not your place to respond—not if you want to keep your women friends, that is.

So, get a little deaf and pleasantly stupid when a friend's husband launches into an anecdote about how fabulous his vegetable garden is, or how highly his boss thinks of him. Don't ply him with questions about his tomato growing techniques or ask for information about fertilizer. Don't act knowledgeable or even interested in his company's bottom line—your interest may be interpreted by his wife (your best friend) as *flirting*. Even if the husband knows you're simply reciprocating his attempts to cheer you up, his wife may think differently.

After all, you're newly single, you're available, and you're right there, in the house. Your dear woman friend, whom you've known for 20 years, may think twice about extending you another weekend invitation, and you don't want that to happen, do you?

Guidelines for Dealing with Other Women's Husbands

1. Don't initiate hugs with other women's husbands. If a husband gives you a big hug as you enter or leave their house, make sure you hug your woman friend afterward—even if you have to walk back into the house to do it.

2. Avoid excessive eye contact with the other women's husbands—it only takes two seconds for a fantasy

to develop, and you don't want to be involved in any fantasies (other than your own).

3. If you're meeting a woman friend for lunch, and you know her husband "likes" you, suggest meeting your friend at the restaurant, rather than at her house where her husband is likely to be hanging out.

4. Avoid wearing anything low-cut, and overly short or tight when dining at the home of married friends. Go for a nice business-casual look.

5. Remember, you can always chew a clove of garlic if things get awkward!

Chapter Forty-Four

Dealing With the Thing
You Don't Want to Deal With

This is the last chapter I'm writing, even though it is not the last chapter in this book. I guess writing about the "thing you don't want to do" is almost as hard as doing it. (Probably not. Probably writing is easier. I have not yet dealt with "the thing you don't want to deal with," so I really don't know.)

We all have it, us widows—that one icky, unpleasant task that, no matter how many times it appears on a list, doesn't seem to get done. Maybe it's a storage unit. Maybe it's a garage, an old car, or even, heaven forbid, more of your husband's closet. You know what it is, and you know how much you don't want to tackle it.

For me, it was my husband's business building. I've described this building before: a two-story house packed with 30 years of business "stuff." I'd been making attempts at cleaning it out since the first month—now, a year after Jack's death, it was still there, waiting for me in all its disarray. I just couldn't seem to face it.

It is not uncommon for a widow or widower to be faced with this situation. Having talked with both sexes, I've learned that most of us have this "dark hole" we can't seem to handle—it corresponds uncannily with a "hole" in our completeness as a healthy person. We try to "go there" but we can't, not yet. It is unpleasant, even scary. After several attempts in the first few months, I just tabled the thing completely. (We're allowed to do that, remember?)

Then in November, about 10 months into my widowhood, I made another pass at it. This was about the same time I started dancing; in fact, I remember thinking, as midnight rolled around and I was still on the dance floor, "Oh! I've got workers coming at 9 a.m. tomorrow!" The workers were a crew of four guys hired by my neighbor, Doc, who was helping me get the building cleaned up. I hired Doc, and he hired the guys and told them what to do; this way, I was in a sort of safe zone, protected from my feelings.

You may need to do something to put yourself in the safe zone when you're tackling "the thing you don't want to do." It's hard to even talk about it, much less do it, but having a trusted friend or neighbor organize this for you helps. Because, let's face it, what you're probably doing is, in some way, getting rid of your husband's stuff.

So my recommendation is—put it off, until you've made an adjustment—either you've started a new job, started seeing someone else (however casually), or taken a major trip—or all three. Don't force yourself to deal with that icky, awful task until you're completely ready.

At this point, almost a year into my widowhood, I have the building about one-fourth cleaned out. It's a slow process, even with five helpers, but it's underway. I no longer cry when I go into that building, I just shut my eyes—figuratively—and forge ahead. I know that the dark spot in my consciousness has to be cleaned out before I can fill it with something new and wonderful.

Guidelines for Dealing With the Thing You Don't Want to Deal With

Just one (and I reiterate)—don't do it until you're ready.

Chapter Forty-Five

Travel

I step out of the pool at the Best Western Seven Seas hotel and walk over to my lounge chair, feeling the warm sun on my shoulders. I'm visiting my brother Robert in San Diego for Christmas, and have been blessed with 70 degree weather during the day. With a sigh, I settle into the lounger, don my sunglasses and close my eyes. I am on vacation, and it's wonderful.

Of all the healing remedies I can recommend to a widow, travel has got to be at the top of the list. When we travel, we remove ourselves from the locked-in mindset that defines our everyday activities: "It's Monday, and I must...clean the house, or go back to work, or do the laundry, or plan the Church bazaar." All of these are worthwhile and necessary activities, but when we travel they lose their quality of critical necessity.

Yes, we think drowsily, lying on our lounge chair, I'm going to re-write that proposal for the boss to highlight its cost-effectiveness...zzzzz. We've dozed off for a moment, to awaken to the sight of a gorgeous pink flower, capturing our attention as no proposal can.

When we travel, we become someone else, however briefly, a someone who is unfettered by cares and obligations and even relationships. As a widow of one year, you may find this shedding of the skin more than typically invigorating. Although I heartily recommend short trips to nearby locales from the very beginning of your widowhood, the long trip, with no chance of turning back, has a unique potential of its own.

Two or three thousand miles from home, we can examine with compassion and respect that widow who has gone through a year of turmoil. Sitting in the sun on a pool deck, we can view ourselves dispassionately, and "catch our breath." Travel is important to everyone, but to a widow, faced with a myriad of choices and new directions, I'd say it's essential.

It is hard to forget our widow status, isn't it? Every memory of our husband brings it back; each time we see a happy couple, we wish we were with *him* again. Yet, away from home, that "widow" identity softens a bit. Lying on a lounge chair, we could be anyone—a career woman at a corporate conference or a famous actress in disguise (hence our dark sunglasses). We could be a gay divorcee, a scientist on a mission, or a spy.

For a widow who has spent a year trying to discover who she is, such role-playing is intriguing and liberating. We begin to realize that the lingering fetters of our widowhood have been in our mind all along—no one wants us to suffer and there is no reason why we should.

The sun hitting my thigh at the point where it joins my hip reminds me of Jack: he liked that area of my body. Now there is a new person in my life who may or may not like it, who will probably have tastes and preferences of his own. Temporarily 3000 miles away from Alan, the possibilities for our connection seem endless—isn't that what we usually feel when we travel?

Later this afternoon, my brother and I will take a ride up the coast to La Jolla, a pretty town north of San Diego. Maybe I'll do some shopping, or maybe not—in any event, we will probably get to see the fabulous West coast sunset over the Pacific Ocean riding back. It's December, and sunset will come early.

But hey, I'm on vacation, and I've got another day.

Guidelines for Travel

1. Choose the best accommodations you can afford—this is no time to scrimp.

2. While you may have an image of yourself from earlier days, hitting the road without a destination or reservations, a planned trip might be best for your first major widow excursion. Remember, you are still somewhat fragile, and you don't need to confront the possibility of "no room at the inn" on your travels.

3. If you travel during the holidays, be super-cautious about *time*. As a widow and possibly a house-bound caregiver, you may not have been in an airport recently. The procedures will probably take twice as long as you remember.

4. Arm yourself with your favorites while traveling: book, notebook, bubble bath, and even a little candy. This is the time to indulge.

5. Travel just as often as you possibly can. Every trip will renew you and give you strength.

Chapter Forty-Six

The Awakening

What does it mean to be alive? As a new widow, you have probably wondered, at times, if you still were. In proportion to the degree of co-dependency you had with your husband, there may have been moments when you felt you were existing in a limbo, half here on earth, and half in a zone of sleep or numbness: not pleasant—but almost a protection against pain and a shield from the realization that you've been left alone in life without your husband.

Some widows get mad at their husbands for dying. Irrational, yes, but quite common; one widow told me her anger toward her beloved did not really subside until she married another man. Even if we don't go that far, we may feel a sort of resentment, as time goes on, toward our state of widowhood—"why is *she* happy with a husband, while *I'm* now a widow?"

This is not a state we want to indulge for long. There are too many wonderful things left to see and do in life to let anger or resentment get the best of us. The antidote, of course, is love. Love in all its many forms—love of self, love of your fellow man, love of God, and sexual love—is a remedy to move you from the state of being "stuck" in widowhood to embracing your new status as an opportunity for growth.

The move into the sunlight of love is an awakening of sorts. We look in the mirror and see a face we know, at last— a pretty face, with a little smile of hope on her lips. We step outside our house, with an awareness of our walk—head held high, hips moving smoothly like an eager teenager—yes, we *are* still here on earth, feeling the energy in our newly toned bodies as we move.

We get in our car and make a call on our cell phone, feeling the air brush past our lips as we speak. Perhaps the call is to a friend we are meeting for lunch at a favorite restaurant. As we laugh and talk, a feeling of happiness surges through us. The day is beautiful, and we will soon be sitting outside on a patio, sipping iced tea and eating a salad of seafood, cherry tomatoes, crisp lettuce, goat cheese and mandarin oranges.

Perhaps the call is to a potential lover; maybe we are planning a rendezvous, and our heart skips a beat as we converse, thrilled at our own courage. How dare we break out of this mold of sadness and embrace life again! How dare we think of sex, a warm embrace, or a kiss? Yet we dare, and we know it's good, not bad—we are alive, and making plans to live with all its risks, its joys, and its inevitable complications.

This is the awakening—a return to the world as you know it and as you are free to invent it in your newly re-born state. Look at widowhood, as your grieving subsides, as a jumping off place—an opportunity to place yourself in the world at the exact point you'd like to be. Maybe you've been thinking about this for several months: you want a new job, a new house, a new life. A year has gone by, so you know your decision is not just a reaction to your husband's death. Instead, it is a reflection of the new "you" who has been steadily gaining strength as you have nurtured yourself. Now you are ready to step out of your nest and fly.

Guidelines for the Awakening

1. Once you realize you are about to emerge from grieving, don't hold yourself back. Even if you are still receiving emails from friends, assuming you are still in

mourning, you alone know when it is time to cease. It's not that you have stopped loving your husband—not at all! But you now feel a fresh pull toward life. It's a pull you can't resist, nor should you.

2. Experiment with cutting the cord. I've begun transferring my wedding ring to the right hand, just as my friend Liz instructed. Yes, I am moving it back and forth now, but I know eventually where it will stay.

3. Encourage every form of new activity that projects you into a new life: a new job, a new lover, even a new haircut will help you see yourself in a new "healed" way.

4. Yes, we want to use caution—but if you've had a year to think about what you really want, chances are you now know what that is.

5. Seize the moment. Possibly there has never been a time in your life when you were so ready and able to live in the present, without worrying too much what the future might bring. The future? From the perspective of widowhood, the future is now. This is a gift from God, so be grateful.

Chapter Forty-Seven

Sleeping on One Side of the Bed

When Jack and I moved to Florida in the winter of 1990, we felt as if we were entering a dream. It was January, but the weather was balmy: 75 degrees in the daytime, cooling down to 60 at night. We set up our house in beachside Daytona quickly and spent hours in bed—sleeping, watching TV, and having sex. Jack and I had just gotten back together after 10 years apart (during which time I'd married and divorced someone else). We had lots to catch up on, and much of that catching up seemed to go on under the covers.

I'll go into the possible benefits of sex on widowhood momentarily, but first, I want to explore the element of sleeping—more specifically, sleeping on one side of the bed. Those first months in Florida, we slept a lot. I seem to recall us waking up at six or seven, rolling over for a hug, then going back to sleep for two or three more hours. After 22 years in New York, the reality of sleeping, undisturbed by blaring horns, fire engines, police sirens and trucks making their weird little back-up noises, was too good to pass up.

Jack and I each had our own side of the bed—mine was on the right (from the point of view of lying on my back), and Jack's was on the left. Twenty plus years later, I am still sleeping on that side of the bed—I have not yet made the transition into the middle. I can't. Sleeping on the right side of the bed means I still have a man of my own, who is waiting to take me in his arms and hold me and kiss me and possibly make love to me. Sleeping in the middle of the bed means there is no such possibility—that I am, however free, a woman alone, who is not going to have sex now or anytime soon.

So I hold out, however irrational it may seem, somehow feeling the presence of my husband still in bed, especially in the early morning on weekends, when I wake up and roll over, wishing for my husband's warm body, then allow myself to drift back to sleep.

Lately in those early morning hours, I have touched myself gently, thinking of this man or that, usually the man I have begun to see regularly, because I am attracted to him. There, I have said it: I am attracted to another man, and when I look at Jack's picture on my little bookmark, I see (or fantasize that I see) an encouragement of sorts, a little "go for it, baby."

Of course that's just my own encouragement, but knowing my husband as well as I did, it would not be out of character for him. Not long before he passed away, we were doing some errands together and he remarked that I "wouldn't have any problem" when he was gone from this life, and he gave me his little knowing smile. So I feel that, if he did know, Jack would be more than accepting of my burgeoning sexual desire—he would encourage it.

And I guess I do need encouragement. Each step I take in the direction of desire is a landmark—an awaking to the inner realization of who I am: a widow of one year, who is interested again in having a man touch her, who wants to experience orgasms, and yes—a woman who wants to gratify the sexual desire of another.

Sex is giving. At the beginning of this book, I gave two rules for survival: one of them was, in essence, to *give* something to someone else. When we engage in sex in the purest sense, we are involved in giving pleasure, affection and gratification to another person. The more unselfishly we can do this, the more complete is our satisfaction. If we engage in sex with the idea of giving, rather than just receiving pleasure, sex can be part of our healing.

Engaged in giving pleasure, we consider the other person's needs. We strive to make that "other" a part of us—our communication becomes imperative. We hold another soul closely, for however long we are together. That giving can be sublime.

I make no move to sleep in the middle of the bed, because, spiritually, I am hoping to be awakened again to the mystery of sex, and for this to happen, I need to make a little room in my consciousness for that "other" person—that man on the left side of the bed.

Guidelines for Sleeping on One Side of the Bed

1. If you find yourself reluctant to move out of your position on one side or the other, take a moment to examine your feelings. What is it you are trying to hold on to?

2. If the answer is intimacy, touch, or the possibility of sex (however subliminal), don't force yourself into the middle of the bed. Your "feeling" self may have other ideas.

3. This is a matter for you, and you alone, to explore. Don't be influenced by anyone (me included, certainly), on whether or not you could or should want sex with another. If you do, please allow yourself to believe that your husband would probably approve.

4. Everything in this area should be handled gently and slowly.

5. Don't feel guilty for thinking about yourself with another man.

Chapter Forty-Eight

Welcome to You!

It has been a year since your husband's passing, a year of grieving, growth and discovery. You have a better idea of who you are now—perhaps better than you've ever had before. During this year of discovery you have walked a tightrope between expressing your feelings and holding them back. You've started projects and not finished them, but perhaps you've completed some old projects that have been hanging around for years. You've deepened your appreciation of friends, and maybe made some new ones. You've also learned to appreciate time spent alone.

During this year you've made a sentimental, sometimes painful, journey through your love life with your husband, pausing to reminisce over pleasing moments when the two of you were very much in love. Perhaps some of those moments came toward the end of his life, bringing a bittersweet remembrance of your time together. And yes, some of those moments have brought tears to your eyes—you've shed a lot of tears this year, dear widow, but it was necessary, and you should have no regrets.

During this year of growth and discovery, you've re-connected with some of your own personal tastes and preferences; you've re-entered the kitchen and learned how to cook for yourself once again; maybe you've resuscitated an old hobby or artistic talent. You've developed an exercise routine not just because you want to stay fit, but because you like the feel of your body in motion. You've learned the importance of getting out of your head and into a relationship with your physical form.

Perhaps you've learned, as the year winds down, that you can still express desire, that wonderful life-giving element bestowed upon humans that makes us conscious of our sexual thoughts toward another. If you have received this gift, I'd say you are blessed.

Even if you haven't yet experienced a re-awakening of desire, who is to say that you won't tomorrow, or the next day, or the next? The process of growth begun during widowhood does not end with the first year. Like a plant reaching for sunlight, your inner life will continue to expand as you stretch yourself to new levels of accomplishment and new vistas of imagination. The solo journey begun in your widowhood may not remain solo, but if you are wise, you will never lose the knowledge gained this year: that you are a self-sustaining individual, capable of re-creating a new life for yourself. You are a whole and complete woman, who is not dependent upon a man for happiness. You are strong, creative and confident, and even if you decide to give yourself to another, for a day or for the rest of your life, a part of you will always retain the ultimate knowledge of *who you really are.*

Welcome to *you*, dear widow. The journey is just beginning.

Guidelines for Welcoming *You*

1. As your first year of widowhood ends, you may be amazed at how well you've coped, and wonder if you've left something out. You haven't. You may ask if you've grieved sufficiently. You have.

2. Continue the guidelines that have brought you to this moment of revelation in your life. When you've got a good thing going, you certainly don't want to stop it.

3. Keep stretching yourself to new areas of accomplishment every day. The intuition you have fostered will keep you from undertaking anything that is too hard for you.

4. Certain elements of your survival guide should be maintained for at least another year: journaling, cooking, exercising, and—above all—extreme nurturing. Any other elements that you feel particularly drawn to should also be continued.

5. Continue to be grateful for all you have learned during your first year of widowhood.

Appendix

25 Ways to Know You're Healed

1. You can look in the mirror and recognize your face as someone you know and like.

2. You can enjoy little things, like making yourself a cup of coffee in the morning, smoothing hand cream on your hands, or arranging pillows on your sofa.

3. You can look at your husband's photograph with affection, but no pain.

4. You feel grateful for the life you are leading and its endless possibilities.

5. You can engage in an activity you used to enjoy with your husband, such as watching a sunset or cooking a favorite meal, and not experience regret.

6. You start to project where you will be next month, next year, or in five years—and you're curious about it.

7. You can talk about your husband with a friend without getting teary-eyed.

8. You can visit a favorite place you and your husband used to frequent, and enjoy it.

9. You start to refer to your husband by his given name in your mind, and not a nameless part of you.

10. You look forward to weekends instead of dreading them.

11. You are starting to lose weight (if that's what you need to do).

12. You are starting to gain weight (if that's what you need to do).

13. You are beginning to differentiate between what you really want to do, and what you think you should do.

14. Friends start to tell you you're doing well.

15. Friends start to compliment your outfit, your smile, or your overall appearance.

16. You don't need friends to tell you that you look good—you know it.

17. If you fall back into a state of moroseness, you know it's only temporary.

18. You are beginning to enjoy things you used to do "long ago," such as dancing, bowling, camping, or baking bread.

19. You no longer fear traveling.

20. You no longer fear staying home by yourself.

21. You no longer fear much of anything. (Good for you!)

22. You find yourself humming or whistling at odd moments.

23. You no longer worry about when you'll finish the closet or complete the "thing you don't want to do." (It'll get done.)

24. You are able to read a book for at least 30 minutes and focus on it.

25. You can go from one activity to another without necessarily referring to a list.

I'd say if you can identify with any 10 of these, you are pretty much healed; 15 or 20, you're ready for take-off; all 25, write your own widow book!

New List of Nice Things to Do

1. Buy a new journal
2. Plan a trip to Key Largo
3. Swim at the Y
4. Walk on the beach
5. Go to church on Sunday
6. Lunch at Topaz
7. Clean sheets
8. Buy new blue pens
9. Be fearless!
10. Visit DeLand Reading Room
11. Lunch at Atlantis Bistro
12. Get together with Anne
13. Call Carole to set up lunch in Mt. Dora
14. See the movie "Heartbreaker" at the Cinematique
15. Plan a trip to California

(from Journal, 1/30/11)

New List of Nice Things to Do

1. Visit Seashore National Park
2. Make reservations for the weekend of July 4
3. Swim at the Y
4. Clean sheets
5. Walk on the beach
6. Lunch at Lulu's
7. Work on novel
8. Buy new blue pens

9. Call Carole re: Sat. 6/4

10. Church on Wednesday and Sunday

11. Take gray silk jacket to cleaners

12. Lunch at Dish

13. Visit DeLand Reading Room

14. Drive north on A1A

15. Visit Orlando Museum of Art

16. Get new books at the library

17. Get ice cream at Cowlicks or NSB

18. Eat lobster bisque at Heavenly

19. See a movie: "Midnight in Paris"

20. Buy cute salt and pepper shakers

(from Journal 5/29/11)

Accomplished in February

1. Swim at Y (1,2,3,4,5,6)

2. View 3 venues for Michelle's play

3. Begin cleaning bedroom

4. Begin cleaning office

5. Finalize pre-paid cremation (for me)

6. Walk on beach (1,2,3,4,5)

7. Send out clippings with obituary: 1 (Paul) 2 (Fred) 3 (Sally)

8. Jack's storage unit cleaned out

9. Wheels balanced on Hyundai

10. Send copy of pre-paid cremation form to Robert

11. Wonderful mini-trip to Cocoa Beach

12. Deposit $1000 in Regions

13. Send out clippings: 4 (Carole) 5 (Victoria) 6 (Marilyn)

14. Do recommendation letters for Courtney and Monique

15. Payment plan set up with Halifax Hospital

(from Journal, 2/4/11)

Accomplished in June

1. Walk on beach (1,2,3,4,5,6,7,8)

2. Swim at the Y

3. Sent condolence note to Mabel

4. Intro and Ch. 1-4 of book accepted by Karen

5. Buy chocolate pie for Doc's return from hospital

6. Do recommendation letter for Anastashia Cartright

7. Email Ch. 5-10 to Karen—accepted 6/10

8. Complete typing novel Ch. 26, 27, 28, 29

9. Close out Jack's two SunTrust accounts

10. Visit Atlantic Center for the Arts—get materials 6/21

11. Email Ch. 11-18 to Karen—accepted 6/18

12. Email new email address to Division of Real Estate

13. Anastashia Cartright is accepted into grad school

14. Buy air filter

15. Karen accepts Ch. 19-26

16. Close out DVS utility account

17. Dust living room, buy pillows

18. Donate Jack's computer to Women's Museum

19. Good meeting with Stefanie Walsh Tues. 6/14

20. Fixed printer

(from Journal 6/2/11)

Things Yet to be Done

1. Replace air filter in dining room
2. Fix fluorescent light in bathroom
3. Call Robin at Liberty Tax Service re: revised MetLife
4. Call St. Louis cemetery re: marker
5. Lock up VA material in strong box
6. Investigate tax exemption for 300 Revilo
7. Do Broker's Continuing Education
8. Pack up more of Jack's clothes
9. De-activate Daytona Video at sunbiz.org
10. Clean out 179 E. International Speedway
11. Sell/give away Jack's equipment
12. Oil change for Hyundai
13. Make a schedule for housecleaning
14. Pay Broker's and Instructor's license fees
15. Explore New York trip

(from Journal 6/1/11)

New List of Scrumptious Things to Do

1. Dinner at Malibu Grill in Pt. Orange
2. Clean sheets
3. Take a little vacation
4. Swim at Y with the sun shining
5. Lunch at Topaz
6. Drive North on A1A
7. Sit in the sun, poolside in deck chair
8. Walk on beach at sunrise

9. Lunch or dinner with a friend

10. Shop at Coldwater Creek

11. Sunday morning in bed

12. Sunday morning in Church

13. Visit to Deland Reading Room

14. Lunch at Atlantis Bistro

15. See a movie

16. Write in journals

17. Writing lunch

18. Room service

19. Lunch after Church at Riverview Grill

20. Visit Women's Museum in DeLand

21. Wear Angel perfume

22. Meditation

(from Journal 2/13/11)

List of Current Blessings

1. Exquisite care and protection from God

2. Demonstrations of God's love everywhere

3. Jack's memorial service was beautiful

4. Friends are thoughtful and kind

5. Unexpected blessing of Michelle's play

6. Robert coming to stay with me for two weeks.

7. Jack's insight in putting my name on bank accounts

8. Wonderful mini-trip to Key Largo

9. Ability to write education article in January

10. House is comfortable and warm

11. Hyundai is fantastic! Miracle car!

12. Doc is very helpful and kind

13. My health is holding up

14. Great swim at the Y on Jan. 28

15. Church four times—healing

16. Reading Room shows glimpses of abundance

17. Gifts and cards from people

18. Beautiful sailboat urn

19. Painting of "reality water lily" from Tom

20. Dinner with Helen at Ronin's

(from Journal, 2/2/2011)

List of Current Blessings

1. Day-by-day closeness with God

2. Increasing demonstrations of God's care

3. God took care of Jack's arrangements

4. Two courses to teach at the college in the fall

5. Wonderful swims and sunning at the Y

6. My comfortable, cozy house

7. Loving, supportive friends

8. Support from Robert, Mary Jo and family

9. Hyundai is miracle car

10. My writing lunches

11. Able to give Jack's clothes to AmVets

12. Meeting with Jeff at VA on 5/25

13. DeLand Reading Room

14. Inspiring Church on Sunday

15. Ability to walk on beach whenever I want

16. New clothes: silk jacket, straw handbag

17. My fabulous Easter vacation
18. Volunteer activity: college alumni association
19. Able to continue writing novel with a plan
20. Karen's book project

(from Journal 5/12/11)

Desires of the Heart

1. Peace
2. Ability and desire to help others
3. Gratitude to God
4. Clarity of mind
5. Able to enjoy life
6. Remember Jack with love
7. Put Jack's affairs in order
8. Put my affairs in order
9. Make right decisions
10. Seek beauty and find it
11. Continue writing
12. Go more deeply into spirituality
13. Seek the kingdom of heaven
14. Volunteer where needed
15. Straighten out finances
16. Communicate with friends
17. Help Robert and Mary Jo
18. Clean the house
19. Continue swimming/walking
20. Take little trips

(from Journal, 1/16/11)

Index

A

affirmation 48
aging 132, 148, 149
Aging 147, 149
Alzheimer's 52
AmVets 13, 151, 218
angels 109
Auntie Mame 171
awakening 199, 200

B

Barefoot Contessa 38
Barnes & Noble 6
Beatles 131, 132, 148, 167
Bell, James Stuart 82
birthday 81, 82, 83, 104, 150, 185, 186, 187, 189
Birthday, His 185, 187
birthdays 83, 150
birthday, your 81, 83, 149
Blessings, List of 45, 46, 47
Boston Market 37
budget 37, 75, 105, 106, 107

C

caretaking 102, 103
car, husband's 23
Caribbean Jack's 32
Child, Julia 38

Christmas 4, 152, 174, 185, 195
closet, husband's 21, 135, 151, 186, 193
Coldwater Creek 43, 82, 106, 174, 217
comfort 5, 6, 15, 33, 45, 46, 98, 123, 148, 152, 156, 165, 173, 187, 189
computer 13, 19, 46, 49, 50, 51, 53, 55, 78, 117, 172, 215
confidence 12, 111, 121, 143, 144
cooking 37, 38, 39, 40, 66, 85, 86, 144, 209, 211
Cosmopolitan magazine 3
crying 5, 27, 28, 29, 42, 61, 93

D

dating 177, 179
death 28, 31, 35, 59, 91, 101, 102, 105, 116, 128, 143, 147, 148, 156,
        157, 160, 186, 193, 200
depression 16, 58, 59, 98, 103, 160
desires, your 19, 23, 24
Diet, Leave 1/3 6, 98, 99
dinner 6, 7, 13, 24, 32, 33, 37, 38, 40, 41, 48, 49, 60, 79, 87, 99, 106,
        124, 131, 161, 167, 168, 172, 187, 189, 216, 217, 218
Dragonfly 33, 81
dressing up 12

E

emotions 5, 15, 24, 27, 29, 77, 116, 121, 140, 153, 155, 171, 172
exercise 10, 98, 101, 137, 139, 181, 182, 183, 207

F

Facebook 51, 52, 86, 89, 90, 91, 131, 148
fashion 97, 148, 149
father 16, 46, 57, 58, 59, 105, 106
finances 21, 108, 219
flirting 190

G

God 28, 34, 45, 53, 54, 61, 101, 107, 160, 199, 201, 217, 218, 219
gratitude 4, 9, 10, 12, 46, 167, 219

grief 5, 12, 16, 21, 37, 49, 50, 52, 53, 57, 59, 61, 98, 102, 116, 136,
        139, 182
grieving 11, 15, 17, 34, 52, 57, 59, 61, 67, 93, 95, 97, 103, 104, 136,
        140, 148, 153, 159, 162, 172, 173, 200, 207
guilt 21, 58, 59, 73, 101, 102, 103, 104, 115, 159, 160, 161

H

healing 10, 12, 23, 28, 47, 53, 54, 91, 110, 115, 116, 121, 124, 125,
        140, 144, 155, 157, 172, 174, 182, 183, 186, 195, 205, 218
health 35, 38, 40, 60, 102, 106, 135, 136, 137, 160, 183, 218
Hibbel, Edna 156
holiday 41, 43, 83, 173, 187
holidays 37, 81, 175, 186, 187, 197
hospital bills 11, 20
house 5, 12, 17, 20, 21, 22, 23, 31, 32, 34, 52, 58, 74, 81, 99, 107, 109,
        115, 156, 173, 189, 190, 191, 193, 195, 200, 203, 217, 218, 219

I

illness, "mirroring" 136
insomnia 160, 161
Internet 7, 86, 93, 106, 131, 140, 149
iPhone 10, 75, 78, 131, 133

J

Jabez prayer 45, 46, 47
job, full-time 105, 153, 162, 173, 186
job, part-time 107, 108
journal 6, 12, 13, 19, 46, 50, 53, 54, 55, 56, 67, 78, 83, 86, 117, 127,
        149, 155, 160, 185, 213, 214, 215, 216, 217, 218, 219

K

Kennedy, Jackie 27, 28

L

lists 3, 10, 16, 24, 55, 77, 78, 79, 172, 174, 175
loneliness 85, 86, 87, 109
looks, your 97, 99
Lord's Prayer 46
love 5, 16, 17, 28, 29, 31, 37, 38, 42, 55, 58, 60, 67, 74, 76, 79, 89, 102, 103, 109, 110, 115, 124, 125, 148, 150, 156, 157, 161, 166, 167, 168, 179, 182, 199, 204, 207, 217, 219
lunch 7, 13, 17, 35, 39, 41, 42, 48, 50, 52, 73, 74, 75, 77, 81, 93, 98, 99, 106, 120, 161, 191, 200, 213, 214, 216, 217

M

mantra 139, 140
masturbation 128, 129
meditation 137, 139, 140, 141, 217
memorial service 3, 9, 11, 17, 19, 20, 27, 53, 119, 147, 217
memories 15, 21, 29, 123, 124, 125
Metropolitan Museum of Art 43
mistakes 93, 95
money 6, 9, 23, 54, 105, 106, 107, 110, 166
mother 15, 16, 17, 57, 59, 106, 128

N

Nice Things to Do 15, 16, 17, 55, 213
NO-FLY zone 32
nurturing yourself 15, 17, 28, 121

P

Pandora 131, 132, 133, 168
phone time, unlimited 6
photographs 10, 155, 156, 157
planning 86, 89, 173, 174, 200
Please Stand By 90
prayer 12, 45, 46, 47, 48
Praying from the Heart 82

prepared food 39
probate 20, 21
project 22, 33, 55, 87, 109, 110, 111, 144, 145, 159, 168, 186, 211, 219

R

Ray, Rachel 38
reiki 109
reincarnation 109
repairs 69, 71, 77, 107
Rise and Shine 139

S

Seashore National Park 115, 152, 186, 213
self-esteem 6, 140, 144, 159
serendipity 71, 122
sex 10, 40, 127, 128, 129, 149, 167, 200, 203, 204, 205
Sex and the City 149
sexual fantasies 127, 128, 129, 167
Shepherd, Cybill 185, 186
shopping 16, 17, 24, 51, 52, 85, 101, 106, 149, 150, 152, 186, 196
social 20
social security 20, 106
superwoman 43, 49, 51, 52, 71
survival, rules for 9, 12, 204

T

tears 10, 27, 28, 29, 37, 42, 60, 90, 94, 103, 132, 157, 167, 173, 185, 186, 187, 207
therapy 59, 103
time, alone 31, 117
Topaz Hotel 73
Transcendental Meditation 139
travel 28, 32, 34, 195, 196, 197
treats 28, 38, 65, 82
trending 149

V

vacation 6, 7, 22, 86, 108, 119, 125, 175, 195, 197, 216, 219
Valentine's Day 41, 42, 43
Veteran's Administration Center 95
Vietnam 95, 151

W

wedding ring 73, 124, 125, 165, 166, 178, 180, 201
widow's rule of thumb 21
Wilkinson, Bruce 47
women's empowerment movement 9
women's group 34
work capacity 121

Y

youth 148, 150

Other Books by MSI Press

Achieving Native-Like Second-Language Proficiency: Speaking

Achieving Native-Like Second-Language Proficiency: Writing

A Believer-in-Waiting's First Encounter with God

Blest Atheist

Communicate Focus: Teaching Foreign Language on the Basis of the Native Speaker's Communicative Focus

Diagnostic Assessment at the Distinguished-Superior Threshold

El Poder de lo Transpersonal

Forget the Goal: The Journey Counts...71 Jobs Later

How to Improve Your Foreign Language Proficiency Immediately

Individualized Study Plans for Very Advanced Students of Foreign Language

Losing My Voice and Finding Another

Mommy Poisoned Our House Guest

Puertas a la Eternidad

Road to Damascus

Syrian Folktales

Teaching and Learning to Near-Native Levels of Language Proficiency (Vol. 1-4)

Teaching the Whole Class

JOANNA ROMER

The Rise and Fall of Muslim Civil Society

Thoughts without a Title

Understanding the People Around You: An Introduction to Socionics

What Works: Helping Students Reach Native-like Second-Language Competence

When You're Shoved from the Right, Look to the Left: Metaphors of Islamic Humanism

Working with Advanced Foreign Language Students

Journal for Distinguished Language Studies (annual issue)

CPSIA information can be obtained at www.ICGtesting.com
Printed in the USA
LVOW071116110113

315308LV00003B/73/P